Rick Apperson has given us an honest and moving narrative of how truly hard it is to find a healthy church in times of cultural captivity. No form or expression of the visible church is left out of his penetrating story, yet he retains hope for the visible church because of the power of Jesus' resurrection. This book could change your life by causing you to alternatively weep and laugh, but then you just might love the church in a new and healthier way in the end.

—John H. Armstrong,
president of ACT 3 and author of *Your Church Is Too Small*

Rick takes the reader through a valley of the shadow of death—only sadly, this valley's shadow is cast by a series of disastrous church experiences. But through, it he freshly encounters Christ and learns that surely goodness and mercy follow him all the days of his life, and he will dwell in the house of the Lord forever. A book for all those who love the church enough to want the best for her.

—Mark Buchanan, www.markbuchanan.net

KILLED BY THE CHURCH, RESURRECTED BY CHRIST

RICK APPERSON

WESTBOW·
PRESS
A DIVISION OF THOMAS NELSON
& ZONDERVAN

Unless otherwise indicated, all Scripture quotations are from The Holy Bible, English Standard Version® (ESV®), copyright © 2001 by Crossway, a publishing ministry of Good News Publishers. Used by permission. All rights reserved.

Scriptures marked NKJV are taken from the New King James Version. Copyright © 1982 by Thomas Nelson, Inc. Used by permission. All rights reserved.

Scriptures marked NIV are taken from The Holy Bible, New International Version®, NIV® Copyright © 1973, 1978, 1984, 2011 by Biblica, Inc.™ Used by permission. All rights reserved worldwide.

Scripture quotations marked NASB are taken from the New American Standard Bible®, Copyright © 1960, 1962, 1963, 1968, 1971, 1972, 1973, 1975, 1977, 1995 by The Lockman Foundation. Used by permission.

Scripture quotations marked NLT are taken from the Holy Bible, New Living Translation, copyright © 1996, 2004, 2007 by Tyndale House Foundation. Used by permission of Tyndale House Publishers, Inc., Carol Stream, Illinois 60188. All rights reserved.

Scriptures marked GW are taken from God's Word®. Copyright 1995 God's Word to the Nations. Used by permission of Baker Publishing Group. All rights reserved.

WestBow Press books may be ordered through booksellers or by contacting:
WestBow Press
A Division of Thomas Nelson & Zondervan
1663 Liberty Drive
Bloomington, IN 47403
www.westbowpress.com
1 (866) 928-1240

ISBN: 978-1-4908-5378-9 (sc)
ISBN: 978-1-4908-5377-2 (hc)
ISBN: 978-1-4908-5379-6 (e)

Library of Congress Control Number: 2014917312

Printed in the United States of America.

WestBow Press rev. date: 10/20/2014

CONTENTS

**To the Lord Jesus Christ.
All that I am, all that I do, is because of You.
May this book be used for Your glory.**

A NOTE TO THE READER

Despite the title, this book is not an attack on the church. First, this book is meant as a loving wake-up call to the body of Christ! Second, this book is about perspective and how it changes when one finds his or her identity in Christ. I pray that this book will fulfill those two purposes.

All names of churches have been abbreviated, changed, or generalized. No names have been given for the people involved. Locations of these churches have been mostly ignored, unless there are such overwhelming positive attributes that I want to publicly acknowledge them.

I end the first six chapters with "What I Learned on the Way to the Resurrection." These are items that I draw out of the story, which I feel that the church today should take note of. You will find that I end chapters 8 and 9 with "Things I Learned After the Resurrection."

In addition, each chapter ends with some discussion questions under the heading of "Taking It Deeper" which are designed for personal and/or group use. I also include prayers that you can use as they are or as thought starters, if you so desire.

INTRODUCTION

I guess you could say that I've always had a sort of love/hate relationship with the church. At times, I've loved being a part of the goings-on and felt a real connection. At other times, I've wanted to run away as if the church carried the plague!

I should probably back up here and explain what I mean by the word *church*. Some use this word to describe God's people around the world, who collectively make up the bride of Christ (Revelation 21:9–10). Others use *church* to describe a specific group of people who gather for the purpose of community, worship, and spiritual growth (Acts 2:46–47). For the sake of this book, I'm speaking about the latter.

So with that out of the way, let me tell you a little bit of what this book is about. I chose the title for a reason. Over the years of my faith journey, I, like many others around the world, have been burned by church. I've had some disappointing experiences and sometimes encountered situations that you would expect to read only from a Hollywood screenwriter.

I've also been blessed beyond measure by some amazing churches around the world.

The good, the bad, and the in-between—that's what this story is about. It would have been very easy to toss the baby out with the bathwater and let the issues and problems I encountered in the church chase me away from fellowshipping with others. In fact, for a time it did.

I could also have used these situations as an excuse to walk away from the faith, period. However, God in His mercy kept that from happening. I won't say the whole search for what is authentic and good within the church has been an easy experience. In fact, there have been times when I just wanted to give up. I thank God that He had other plans.

Throughout this book, I'll also include stories of others who have been burned and blessed by their church experiences. I pray you will be encouraged, challenged, and that in the end your faith in God and His church will be strengthened.

Speaking of challenges, let's be honest for just a moment. The church needs a wake-up call. We (the church) need to be aware of what's going on around us and in our congregations. How often do we as a church take our spiritual pulse?

I started paying more attention to the pulse of the church after attempting to memorize the seven letters to the churches found in Revelation 2–3. If we read the seven letters, as recorded there, we find that Jesus' words for the churches were twofold. He spoke about the good things they had done but also pointed out the negatives. He gave them warnings and things to work on. They were encouraged not to rest in the past but to strive to go deeper with Him!

Taking that idea, I've started thinking about my own church experiences, both good and bad. How often does a congregation discuss its problems (aside from the need for a bigger sanctuary or when to have the next "outreach event")? Some aren't aware, or would never admit, that they have any problems to begin with. If anything goes wrong, it must be persecution or an attack from Satan. I don't disagree that Satan wants to destroy God's church, but if we're honest, sometimes we are our own worst enemies.

The actual address to the churches begins in Revelation 1. It's interesting that John starts his letter in Revelation 1:4 with the word *grace*. This to me sets a good tone. What would happen if we, having been shown grace and mercy by the work of Jesus on the cross, displayed that same grace to those we encounter on a daily basis?

When we encounter someone in sin, do we go for a stone, or do we first start from a position of grace?

Taking our spiritual pulse isn't a bad thing; ignoring our pulse is! If we don't know how healthy we are, we might just end up DOA!

So the journey begins. As I weave through my checkered church past, you will find, as I mentioned before, an attempt to show both the good and the bad. For many years, I refused to believe that abusive churches had positive attributes as well. Now, I see that God can still use and redeem any situation! I also see that the best churches in the world still have areas of blindness and room for growth.

I guess the underlying theme, the thing I want you to take away from this book the most, is hope! No matter whether you are in a difficult church situation, are in the healing process, or have no idea what I'm talking about, God isn't done with you yet! We're all on a journey.

But for me to tell my story effectively, we have to go back to the beginning.

Enjoy the ride!

CHAPTER 1

In the Beginning

M y earliest memory of church is that of being baptized as a young child in the Catholic Church. I don't remember much, except that we had to dress up and everyone seemed really happy— well, that and some guy sprinkled water on our heads and we didn't have to use a bar of soap! For a child, that was a big deal.

My mom enrolled me into a Catholic kindergarten class and I really loved the experience. I enjoyed the teacher and had lots of friends, but I could have gone without the frequent application of ruler to knuckles that seemed to be the discipline of choice. Around this time, I remember going to one Catholic Church service and falling asleep, thus ending my first foray into this thing called "church."

I don't know what language was spoken in that service— remember I was five—but as a friend wrote to me recently, one problem he had with the Catholic Church was the fact that it used Latin while everyone else spoke a different language.

> The Catholic Church was interesting. The priest would speak in Latin and sing all by himself in Latin. The funny thing was that the majority of the Catholic congregation was Danish.
>
> —A.H.

My mom has often shared the story about how, when she was pregnant with me, she felt me move for the first time. She said that my grandmother had come over for a visit and sang the hymn "Amazing Grace." My mom tells me that when she heard that song, I began moving in her belly. I shared that story at a church service in our local nursing home where one resident corrected me and said it was not a belly, it was a womb!

That song is my all-time favorite hymn to this day. I like to think that something inside me was already responding to God. God said to Jeremiah the prophet, "Before I formed you in the womb I knew you, and before you were born I consecrated you; I appointed you a prophet to the nations" (Jeremiah 1:5). Now, I don't think God is calling us all to be prophets, but I do believe He knew us even before we were formed in the womb. I take comfort in that fact. He is God!

I don't want to get sidetracked from the theme of this book, but Ephesians 1:4–5 goes along with this for me. It says,

> Even as he chose us in him before the foundation
> of the world, that we should be holy and blameless
> before him. In love he predestined us for adoption as
> sons through Jesus Christ, according to the purpose
> of his will.

For me, these verses take on more relevance because I see in my own life how God really wooed me throughout my childhood. I believe God is wooing all of us, but not all of us respond to that love.

We weren't a church-going family, though we were raised to believe in God and that He had a son named Jesus. Though we weren't born-again Christians, being nominally Catholic, we still had a strong belief in God the Father, His Son Jesus Christ, and the Holy Spirit. I just didn't know what it all meant. I had a little red Gideon's Bible I'd gotten in the fourth grade and would occasionally read it, but the words didn't make sense to me. I still cherished that Bible and knew it was important; however, without proper discipleship, nothing took root in my heart.

I remember a parade in Gettysburg, Pennsylvania, where I was living at the time, when I was nine. As one of the floats passed, its occupants tossed out little red Scripture booklets. In the back was a "sinner's prayer." I must have read that booklet hundreds of times and said that prayer again and again. I had no one to explain it to me, and after a while, this prayer was added in with my "Hail Marys" and "Our Fathers."

> A sower went out to sow his seed. And as he sowed, some fell along the path and was trampled underfoot, and the birds of the air devoured it.
> —Luke 8:5

> The ones along the path are those who have heard; then the devil comes and takes away the word from their hearts, so that they may not believe and be saved.
> —Luke 8:12

These two verses describe where I was. I read the words in these booklets, but as I said before, nothing took root. Without someone to come along beside me and explain what I was reading, it didn't make sense. I really could have used a Phillip (Acts 8:26–40)!

As I entered adolescence, I began to look into other areas of spirituality. I had a friend in school who introduced me to palmistry (palm reading). I began to study lifelines and tried to figure out what all those squiggles on our hands meant. I moved on to childish attempts at ESP, which included trying to predict which playing card (out of a deck of fifty-two) would be flipped over next.

My main hobby though was devouring my daily horoscope. I read it faithfully in the newspaper every day. I was so caught up in the meaning of all these things. Coupled with my unnatural fear

3

of death, it's a good thing no one had heard of Prozac back then, because I would have been a prime candidate! Around 1983, there was a story I read somewhere that, due to a planetary alignment, the world could possibly spin off its axis! I vividly recall freaking out about that one! I was twelve years old and was convinced the world was coming to an end.

Oh, the joys of childhood!

I remember passing a big old Catholic church whenever I walked into town to buy comic books and baseball cards. The church seemed ancient and intimidating.

By the seventh grade, I began moving toward a stronger interest in God, while maintaining my daily horoscope practice. I don't recall any specific reason that my thoughts began turning to God, but I know that I felt He could offer peace. Peace was something I felt like I was missing.

Gettysburg was a very—how should I say?—*interesting* town. There were some downright creepy things going on there, and most people swore by the fact that they regularly saw ghosts. My fear of death was joined with a fear of ghosts, and I think this, more than anything else, might have fueled my desire to know God more.

So it was, at the age of thirteen, that I came home one day and declared to my mom that I was going to start attending church. My mom was very encouraging, as she herself had been watching Christian programming for years. Struggling with multiple sclerosis, she watched shows like *The 700 Club* and shared stories of faith and prayer with me when I got home from school. In fact, I remember my first real time of prayer was when my mom and I prayed together for a need in the family.

Again, you may notice this wooing I talked about earlier. No matter how far I wandered in search of a spiritual purpose or meaning for my life, God seemed to always place things in my path to draw my interest back to Him!

I mean, just try handing out Bibles in public school today or throwing Scripture booklets from a parade float! Even my mom's

4

viewing of Christian programming wasn't accidental. She could have gotten caught up in many programs, yet she kept gravitating to religious shows. Despite the bad reputation these types of programs have today, in the late 1970s and early 1980s, they opened us up to learning more about the nature and character of God.

With newfound determination, I began to steel myself to the idea of stepping into a church. Being raised nominally Catholic, I really didn't have any idea where else to go but the Catholic Church, yet I found an excuse not to take the next step every time the opportunity came around. I was intimidated, as the choice seemed huge. Okay, the building seemed huge as well!

Finally, just as I was prepared to go to a service, my family uprooted and moved to Tennessee. My journey into the world of churches was about to get a bit more interesting.

*   *   *

The Smoky Mountains of East Tennessee are quite beautiful. However, life there was nothing like I expected. I had an image in my mind of backwoods rednecks drinking moonshine and sitting around on their front porches spitting. I know it's a stereotype, but when my parents told us we were moving from "civilized" Pennsylvania down to Tennessee, that was the image that sprang to mind. I believe this was because in the Gettysburg of my childhood, everything was focused on the Civil War. I was picturing Johnny Reb still fighting the war. I had often heard that the "South shall rise again!"

I didn't know that the Smoky Mountains and Sevier County receive millions of tourists each year. The Tennessee I encountered was filled with bumper boats, mini-golf courses, a theme park, water slides, hotels, and more traffic than I could shake a stick at.

I was excited by the possibilities. I became even more determined to attend church in our new town. Our phonebook only showed one Catholic church, but it was miles away in another community.

I wasn't sure what to do, but in the weeks ahead, we began to settle into our new home and my siblings and I explored our new neighborhood. That's when the bus lady came for a visit.

I think if done correctly, a bus ministry can open up many doors for children to hear the gospel. Unfortunately, it sometimes becomes all about the numbers and the original intent can get lost in the fixation of "proving" the ministry's worth! Ministry can often take a back seat to stats!

In this case though, I was unaware of any ministry happening. We just knew we had been invited to church. A local independent Baptist church was planning a vacation Bible school and a nice older lady drove around the neighborhoods inviting kids to come. Our parents said yes, and before long, we were on the bus for the first night of VBS.

We pulled up to the church and all the kids piled out, excitedly making their way into the building. I took a seat near the back, just watching and nervously waiting to see what would happen next. The evening was filled with fun songs and activity.

Then it came time for the message and I heard the words that would change my life forever: I was going to hell!

I missed everything else this preacher said after that, except that there was a way out—through Jesus dying on the cross, an act He did out of love for us! One of the Scriptures shared was from Romans 6:23. "For the wages of sin is death, but the free gift of God is eternal life in Christ Jesus our Lord." I was stunned by all of this and stayed glued to my seat when the altar call was given.

I had a fitful sleep that night, wrestling with the implications of my newfound wisdom. I worried, fretted, and turned over in my mind the things the preacher had said. Then I would doze off and wake again only to start the cycle over.

That whole thing about dying and going to hell if I didn't know Jesus as Lord and Savior really got to me. I'm not a fan of scaring people into heaven. I think the truth of heaven and hell should be discussed—and the repercussions of rejecting Christ should be included—but fear shouldn't be used to motivate people into accepting Christ. I think, without proper discipleship, the fear factor creates works-based Christianity and a wrong God concept. In my life, fear played a big part in my initial decision, and the outcome was for a time definitely works based.

Having spent that night wrestling with my thoughts, the next evening I couldn't wait to get to church. When the invitation was given to accept Jesus Christ as Lord, I practically bolted up the aisle. I was taken into a side room with other kids where the gospel was presented to us again to make sure we understood it. Then I bowed my head and repeated a prayer asking Jesus into my heart.

Something happened that night. I felt lighter, freer, and less troubled than I had in a long time. Before I departed, I was given a set of instructions, a sort of biblical to-do list.

1. Read my Bible every day
2. Go to church
3. Share the gospel with others

The list sounded easy. My wake-up call came shortly thereafter.

Our weeklong VBS ended, and before much time had passed, my siblings and parents also committed their lives to Christ.

I began attending this same Baptist church and was soon baptized by immersion. It was all so exciting and new. Being an inquisitive fellow, I decided to look for someone to answer a burning question in my young heart: what happens if we sin after becoming a Christian? The first person I found to answer my question was unfortunately the assistant pastor. His heartfelt, well-thought-out, caring response was that I would go to hell!

Maybe he was joking, maybe not. To a fourteen-year-old new Christian, I was left confused and worried, as I knew I had already blown it. The result of his off-handed comment was a struggle with doubt and fear that I wrestled with for years. Was I really saved? If not, maybe I should say the sinner's prayer over and over when I knew I had done something wrong.

This goes back to my earlier comment about fear leading to works-based Christianity. I felt like I had to perform to gain God's love and approval. My identity wasn't wrapped in Christ but in being a good Christian. I continuously doubted whether I was good enough or accepted. My fear was the antithesis of 2 Timothy 1:7, which says, "For God has not given us a spirit of fear, but of power and of love and of a sound mind" (NKJV).

Years later, God released me from that bondage of doubt.

What I needed was a more mature believer to come along beside me and walk with me for a season—kind of like Paul and Timothy's approach. I needed an older believer, or someone who had been in the faith a bit longer, to mentor me. That's what happened to G. W.

Reality vs. Perception

Sometimes, what is said and how we perceive or "hear" what is said are two different things.

As I said, the pastor's answer could have been a joke, but the way I heard it, in my young searching mind, was as a very real and knowledgeable statement made by someone in authority.

This illustrates the importance of Proverbs 18:21, which says, "Death and life are in the power of the tongue, and those who love it will eat its fruit."

We should bridle our tongue just as the Bible mentions (James 1:26). Our words can impact others for eternity!

Driving into the parking lot of the church on Turner Road, I met the three guys and four girls who would become my summer mentors in my budding faith. I wasn't the only one in the group who hadn't grown up in the church, but while I had been a Christian for days, the others had a few years on me and I thought they were Bible rocket scientists compared to me.

—G. W.

* * *

As my family became more involved in this church, I began hearing more and more rules that seemed to add to the list I had been given that first night.

1. Women should only wear dresses.
2. Swimming with the opposite sex is a sin.
3. Dancing is forbidden.
4. Only Christian music is acceptable to listen to.
5. Only the King James Bible is authorized to read.

That last one was attached to a large bronzed plaque bolted to the wall of the sanctuary. I found out that, according to our leaders, all these rules were there to keep our minds pure and free from sin. It didn't work. I kept thinking about all the stuff I couldn't do, and when I broke a rule, the condemnation was overwhelming.

I did enjoy the church's potluck suppers. Tables were laid out with a variety of hearty dishes and kids were encouraged to run around and have fun playing games like tag and basketball. When everyone had burned off their energy, we would gather together, the pastor would pray, and then we would enjoy a meal together as a congregation. These events were fun and enjoyed by all.

However, trouble was brewing on the horizon. It came shortly after God performed a miracle. Soon our world would be turned upside down.

*   *   *

My mother had been slowly losing her battle with multiple sclerosis over the last decade. Her once healthy body was now weakened and our family didn't expect her to live through the next year. In fact, her doctor had pretty much said that the end was sooner rather than later. She still had faith that she could be healed, and in fact, people in the church had been praying that God would do just that. At least one man from another church was praying too, but that's a story for later.

When the healing came, no one expected it and some didn't know what to do! The healing came late in the night and muscles appeared full and strong where moments before they were small and weak. When I awoke in the morning, my mom was doing toe touches, lifting weights, moving her neck, and even beating me in arm wrestling! My whole family rejoiced at this miracle.

When my mom shared the miracle with our pastor and others, she was told not to talk about it beyond the brief mention on Sunday. We were confused by this, as the church had been praying for the miracle to happen.

During the days after my mom was healed, the assistant pastor had seemed quite resistant to the idea that my mom could have been healed. The kicker came when the assistant pastor came to our house. The same guy who had told me I would go to hell for sinning even after I became a believer now had the audacity to say something far worse to my parents. "Maybe God *didn't* heal you. Maybe Satan did it to cause disruption in your life!"

Well, let me just say that that didn't go over so well. I still don't know how my parents showed the restraint they did. They were shocked and I half-expected my dad to toss this pastor out on his derriere. That was the last straw for our involvement in this particular church.

We were still reeling from the way our church leaders had responded to the healing when we found our new church home.

I mentioned that another man had been praying for mom's healing as well. The day before the miracle, a man showed up at our door from GCC, a church we had never heard of from the next town over. This man stopped by to say that his church had received a call that we needed prayer for our financial struggles. At the time, my family didn't have any financial needs, but while there, he prayed for my mom to be healed.

You may not believe in miracles, and I am not saying everyone who prays will be healed, but I do know what I saw with my own eyes and the experience my family had.

After her healing, my mom called this church and we were invited to visit. Thus began the next leg of my journey through this thing called church.

Already my identity was being shaped. Added into the fear of sinning was my struggle to keep the rules I had been given. I felt like I wasn't good enough and in no way would I allow myself—or anyone else, for that matter—to question the things of God. I had an unspoken image of a sitting on a throne while looking to see whom He could throw lightning bolts at!

I was sure that one false step would send me to hell! My faith was getting ready to be put to the test though. Would I continue to believe in God, or would my future encounters with the church be the death of me?

What I Learned on the Way to the Resurrection

1. Sharing a meal together is extremely important. People tend to relax over a meal and will share more personal stories with those around them.

Have you ever noticed how many times it's recorded in the four gospels that Jesus ate a meal? He fed and ate with the four thousand (Mark 8:1–9) and the five thousand (Luke 9:10–17). He ate a meal with Matthew in his house (Matthew 9:9–19). He called Zacchaeus down from a tree to share a meal in his place of residence (Luke 19:1–10). He ate at Mary and Martha's place (Luke 10:38–42). And of course, we all know about the Last Supper (Matthew 26:26–29).

I think Jesus was setting a good example here. Fellowship and hospitality were on continual display. Some people, the religious leaders of the day for example, didn't always think these meals were a good thing. However, Jesus fellowshipped with those who would have Him and lives were changed. People were impacted through His ministry—over meals.

One of the most powerful meals Jesus shared must have been when He cooked breakfast for the disciples, encouraged them to eat, and later spoke to Peter (John 21).

After Jesus was taken back up into heaven, we see the church starting to grow. In Acts 2:40–47, there's specific mention of how the early church broke bread from house to house. People were happy, sold personal items to share with those who were needy, and got saved! (I never saw *that* at a potluck, but you get the point.)

What is it about a meal?

A meal helps people to relax. They feel comfortable and will open up more. When people open up, they share their hearts, and if we're effective listeners, we can hear how God would have us respond. Maybe it's to provide for a need. It might be just to walk with someone during a time of crisis. Maybe someone needs some encouragement. Whatever the issue, a meal can break down walls.

Having a meal together can also draw us closer to the Father. Notice how many teaching moments came when Jesus ate with someone. The Bible says where two or more are gathered, He is in the midst (Matthew 18:20). What better way to gather than over a meal?

Another fantastic thing about a common meal is that it gives us the opportunity to bless one another. We can follow Christ's command to show hospitality to one another by passing a platter, filling a water glass, or washing dishes.

When a church family eats together, God can take them deeper than they have ever been before. Lives can be touched and people can be impacted for eternity.

So fire up the barbeque, grab a few friends, and *live!*

Taking It Deeper

1. Have you felt the Lord "wooing" you over the course of your lifetime?

2. If so, what did that "wooing" look like?

3. Do you feel, believe, and accept that God loves you? Is there a particular experience in your past that may be hindering you from being able to receive the fullness of His love?

4. Have you ever felt confused or hurt by words other Christians have shared with you?

5. Is there a Bible verse that has been a comfort to you in your journey with the Lord?

Father, I pray that as I read this book, I will allow Your love to heal the hurts from my past. I ask that You will help me not to linger on the pain but to embrace Your love and to even begin to extend Your forgiveness to those who have caused me that pain. In Jesus' name, amen.

CHAPTER 2

A Church by Any Other Name

G CC didn't look anything like the pictures I had associated with "church." There was no steeple and there was no bell to ring. In fact, when we first entered the foyer, I was struck by how much the building differed from other churches I had seen. A beautiful two-story wood building, GCC was only identified as a church by the sign out front.

I wasn't sure what to expect that first Sunday. The people seemed friendly enough. When the worship team came to the front, I was a little taken aback. I had seen choirs and pianists, but never a whole team of musicians. Flutes, drums, and pianos were just the beginning. When the music started, everyone's hands shot up in the air. I remember looking around, trying to figure out who they were waving at. I had never seen

Lift Your Hands

I remember one pastor telling members of the congregation, "It's okay to lift your hands during worship ... It doesn't make you a Pentecostal."

His attempt at humour aside, the Bible does say in Psalm 63:4, "Thus I will bless You while I live; I will lift up my hands in Your name" (NKJV).

anyone praise the Lord by lifting their hands. It was a new experience for me.

Over the next few months, my family fell in love with this church. The pastor was friendly, funny, and caring. People seemed to genuinely want to get to know one another. Concern was expressed about not only the needs of church members but also those of the surrounding community as well. The church community made each family feel special. We felt valued and cared for in whatever circumstance we found ourselves.

The pastor would check in with members individually to see if they had any needs the church could address. On one occasion, a group of people passed through town in the wintertime and their bus broke down. The pastor threw open the doors to the church and let them bed down in the sanctuary.

Looking back on this time, I see a reflection of the church in Acts, in particular the description in Acts 2 of how the people looked out for one another, sharing everything they had.

The worship times were also quite beautiful. There was freedom of expression and no one cared if we dropped to our knees in worship or sang loudly and off-key. Through it all, I felt reverence and awe for the Lord throughout the service. The worship times seemed to linger yet no one was in a hurry to move on in the service.

One thing I thought was neat, though I wasn't involved in it, was that the church ran a school in the lower level of the facility. The church provided a place where homeschooling parents could work together, teaching various subjects and running a full school program from the Christian perspective.

Our period at GCC was an amazing time, and my whole family enjoyed being there. The pastor's messages were relevant and seemed to speak to people right where they were. My parents soon began to discuss the idea of becoming members of the church. As for me, I was all for the idea.

That's when our pastor dropped a bombshell: he was moving. Just as we began to process this news, we were hit with another resignation. Two weeks after the pastor departed, the worship leader felt it was time to move on as well. We were saddened by their departures but felt strongly that the heart of the church would not change.

We were so wrong. Not only did the heart change, but so did the name and everything else.

*   *   *

I was still trying to be a "good" Christian, still struggling with fears while displaying a good public "Christian" face. Many people would comment to my parents about how "good" we were as kids and teens. I was constantly looking for approval and validation that my faith was real, thinking that if other Christians approved, God probably would as well. Or at least, I hoped He would. I wanted to be seen as having it all together (at the age of fifteen). I was sure that if I let my guard down and shared my fears and struggles, the church and God Himself would reject me.

Our church began its pastoral search. The plan, as announced, was to bring in various pastors to preach so that the church members could vote on who they wanted to lead the church. When the first candidate came, he tried to connect with the youth right away. Moving throughout the sanctuary, he handed out gum to each teen and kid. It was a small gesture, but it felt like he was trying to make a connection.

I remember my siblings and I thought the first candidate was cool and relatable. My parents weren't so impressed. They wanted to see the other candidates before making a decision. They never got the chance. The elders decided to forgo any other candidates and voted on this first pastor. He won the vote and, for better or worse, got the job.

Shortly after he was installed as pastor, he decided to establish a new vision and change the name of the church. It seemed like a minor thing at first, yet it was actually a harbinger of things to come.

Change is inevitable when there is new leadership, and not all change is bad. However, change should never be made in a vacuum or just for the sake of change. Some organizations say that new leaders should not change things for a period of time (six months to a year) so that they can get the feel for what is happening, how things work, etc. I have found that to be a good rule of thumb (where possible) over my career in management and ministry.

During this time, I began to feel God might be calling me into missions. I was fifteen and looking for direction as to my future. The pastor called me up one day and asked to meet with me. He said that since I had an interest in missions, I should step into the role of missions director at church. My responsibility would be to contact all of the missionaries our church supported, keep the bulletin boards updated, and share from the pulpit any missionary news that came in. I was excited by this new opportunity. In one sense, this was a great opportunity for me to show that I was a passionate Christian. Surely, as a mission director, God would look more favorably on me. I thought everyone would be as excited about missions as I was.

The pastor loaned me some of his missionary related books and a few impacted my future work on the mission field.[1]

*   *   *

Words are sometimes more powerful than actions, and though his actions seemed to encourage my involvement in ministry, more than once I suffered at the withering words spoken to me by the new pastor. I remember babysitting for him and his wife when they went out one evening. I sat in their living room watching TV with both the kitchen and living room lights on. When the pastor came home, he made a comment about being able to see his house all the way down the road due to all the lights being on. He asked me if I was

---

1   I list these and other books that have impacted my thinking at the end of this book.

afraid of the dark. His tone was mocking and soon his words were too. He made numerous references to my "fear" on the trip back to my house. When he dropped me off, he told my parents I was afraid of the dark and that I had lit up his house like a museum. I was humiliated and angry that someone in authority would do that.

Our church members were encouraged to fill out a spiritual gifting survey. I was excited to fill one out, as I thought it would be great to know where my strengths and weaknesses lay. The excitement lasted only until the pastor called to discuss my results with my mom. Apparently, I had scored highest in the area of compassion, and the pastor made it abundantly clear that scoring high in that area wasn't something he thought should be celebrated or encouraged. I was confused in light of Scriptures like Galatians 6:2, which says, "Carry each other's burdens, and in this way you will fulfill the law of Christ" (NIV). I found compassion and sympathy in numerous Bible verses. I began to wonder if I was misinterpreting them. These thoughts added to my doubt and insecurities in my relationship with God. The pastor informed me that being led with compassion was not how you operate in ministry. A "bleeding heart" was not what was needed. In his opinion, you needed other strengths to be in the forefront.

I began to see compassion being minimized in our church as well. People who would once have given you the shirts off their backs began to worry more about the cost of the shirts. It seemed the wealthier families were being praised from the pulpit when it came time to take up tithes and offerings. The pastor would make mention of kids and teens who gave money in the offering; the only kids mentioned were those of wealthy families. Those families were invited regularly to the pastor's house for dinner. The one time my family was invited, the pastor made mention of how large (five people) our family was and that he couldn't afford anything but soup for dinner when we were there. He never seemed to have a problem inviting larger, wealthier families over though. This was not an issue of jealousy, but it did seem strange that only the wealthy were praised regularly for tithing, giving, helping, etc., and always by name.

Despite the increasing hurts, we continued to persevere through these issues, as we really cared for the people who went to this church. As time went on, however, the pastor's messages seemed to become more direct. He even mentioned once that he had files on each member of the church and knew more about what happened in our families than even we did. I found out firsthand how this came about.

Apparently, our pastor would talk to the kids and teens and grill them about their home lives. My brother and I were both approached this way. Questions ranged from how often we saw our parents pray and read the Bible to whether or not they were "spirit-filled." We were both uncomfortable with this line of questioning and refused to divulge specifics. His continual questions on our home life and how we operated as a family seemed invasive. He never approached our parents with these questions. We began to pay more attention to the warning flags being raised all around us.

* * *

As I grew older, I wanted to go deeper in my walk with the Lord. I attended our youth group for a time, but the services were geared toward the younger kids and I wanted more depth in the material presented. On Sunday nights, there were so many guest speakers, prayer times, and testimonies that I decided to start going to the Sunday night service instead of the youth group. The pastor immediately tried to put the kibosh on that idea. He strongly encouraged me to continue attending the youth group for the sake of the younger kids. When I expressed my desire to do otherwise, he decided to go to my parents to see if they could encourage me to attend youth group instead of the regular service. My parents backed me up, but it wasn't the last time he mentioned how he felt I should be with the youth instead of the adults.

Wednesday nights at GCC had been designed for home groups. Instead of meeting at the church, members would meet in area homes where they talked about Sunday's message, studied the Bible, and prayed for and encouraged one another. There were snacks, fun conversation, and a desire to know God more.

This was one more area that changed within the church. Instead of meeting every week to dig into the Word, groups were encouraged to have more activity times. Bowling and flag football began replacing Bible studies and prayer. It was disconcerting to see how easily everyone went along with these changes.

I don't believe there's anything wrong with playing games as a group; I think Christians can and should get together and enjoy leisurely visits without everything turning into a Bible study. I love fun and games. The problem I noticed was more of a tonal shift. Every ministry under GCC was closed or changed when the new pastor took over. For example, the Christian school program, which had been running for years, was discontinued after the school year ended. Parents weren't happy, but it was explained that we didn't need a school at the church. This program was resumed a few years later, however, when the pastor's daughter reached school age. First a kindergarten was added, with subsequent grades being introduced as their daughter moved up in age.

Another area that was no longer a focus was the benevolence ministry. The church used to have a very vibrant food pantry under GCC and, as previously mentioned, had a major focus on helping church families and people in the community at large. Before long, our church food pantry was nearly empty and people were being turned away while the church continued purchasing newer and more expensive items for the worship team. It seemed our church was no longer focusing on reaching out to people in need.

This became extremely clear when one of the unwed mothers in our church became pregnant for a second time. Instead of walking through a healthy and biblical approach to dealing with a believer who stumbles, this woman was denounced publicly and church members were strongly discouraged from helping her with child care or other basic needs. No one was supposed to reach out to her. When the leadership was approached on this issue, it was made clear that giving her assistance in any form was an act of rebellion to those in leadership.

As I mentioned, there are biblical ways to deal with those who stumble and are caught in sin. Let me step away from my story for a moment to share a letter that was sent to me recently that makes the point better than I can. Unfortunately, the model used in this story was not how our church handled the situation.

> My daughter had a tough time in her teenage years and once made a choice to run away. Several weeks later, the police called to say that they had my daughter. We (my wife and I) drove to get her and bring her home. We found out that a young man from our church had helped her run away. When we had asked our daughter's friends, including this young man, prior to this, they had all denied knowing her whereabouts. It later came out that she had been at this young man's grandparents' house.
>
> Matthew 18:15 says, "If your brother sins against you, go and tell him his fault, between you and him alone. If he listens to you, you have gained your brother." So that's what I did. I met this young man after church one day and asked if I could talk with him. When talking about the situation and his lies, there was no confession of anything.
>
> Matthew 18:16 says, "But if he does not listen, take one or two others along with you, that every charge may be established by the evidence of two or three witnesses." I had my wife and a brother in the Lord visit the young man at his home, inviting his parents to join if they would like. Still there was

no confession or repentance. The goal here wasn't for this young man to apologize to me; it was about this young man being reconciled to Christ.

—R. J.

Did you catch that key statement in the story R. J. shared? The goal for following the biblical approach to correction wasn't to get an apology but to see the young man reconciled to Christ! There is no better reason to speak correction into someone's life. As you will see from the rest of R. J.'s story, the biblical approach bears fruit.

> Following the Scripture, we made an appointment with one of the associate pastors at our church. My wife and I had been praying that there would be a breakthrough and that this young man may be restored in a mighty way. Well, when the young man came in with his dad, he confessed everything and asked for forgiveness—not just mine, but he asked God to forgive him, for that is who the sin was against was: God and God alone.
>
> The beautiful part is that after this, I had the opportunity to love and disciple this young man for a couple of years. He is now in Bible college working on his theology degree and an assistant pastor himself. He is also happily married with a young son of his own.
>
> —R. J.

I praise God for the beautiful redemption found in this story. Redemption should be the key to any church discipline. In fact, any rebuke or correction of a brother or sister in Christ should have redemption at the heart of it. We should always be seeking the restoration and redemption of those who have sinned and/or walked away from God.

* * *

We soon saw the need to leave the church, the wisdom of which was confirmed years later when the church custodian admitted that the pastor had paid him to spy on the members of the church. He had been told to drive by the members' houses, note cars that came and went, follow the members around town, and report back to the pastor all of the places they had gone to and what they did while there. It may sound far-fetched, but it is another possible explanation on how these "files" that the pastor said he kept on everyone came into existence.

When we left the church, so many people stopped talking to us. It was like we had a contagious disease. A friend of mine shared that same thought with me not to long ago. Apparently, I'm not the only one who's had that experience after leaving a church!

> It's just strange how people who are supposed to be Christians totally ignore you or treat you indifferently in public when you aren't fellowshipping with them anymore. If we all truly love Jesus, know we are His servants, and are all headed to heaven one day, why do we treat others like this? This defeats the purpose of church to me.
>
> —S. B.

For my family, there was no going back. The journey through the trials and tribulations of church continued.

Personally, I was beginning to lose some trust in the church. I wouldn't have admitted that though, and numerous times over the years, I even felt guilty for thinking it. I felt even more guilt when I began to doubt God and His faithfulness. The thought *Does*

God really care? rattled in my mind more than once, but whenever someone would ask the why questions in regards to God, I would publicly take the opposite tact and come to God's defense! I was afraid that by letting others give voice to my own doubts, it would make them more real to me. Since I was already feeling like I had blown it spiritually, allowing more doubt to creep in was quite scary to me. I felt unworthy and was losing any joy I had in my relationship with Jesus Christ.

I was slowly developing a shell around my heart, beginning to think I had to do things on my own. I was feeling more and more that I had to earn my salvation, and that meant more and more work: church participation, attempts at evangelism, etc. The works-based mind-set was becoming entrenched.

What I Learned on the Way to the Resurrection

2. Those caught in the act of sin need to hear and see God's grace
   in action.

Who knows what was running through the woman's mind?
As she was dragged into the street where Jesus stood, the Pharisees
began eagerly sharing the woman's sin with Jesus and the people
around Him. The woman had sinned. She had been caught in the
act—the very act!—of adultery.

"Moses said that, according to the law, she should be stoned,"
one of the Pharisees said. "What do you say, Jesus?"

Stooping down, Jesus took His finger and began writing on the
ground.

Again, He was questioned. "What do you say? Should this
woman be stoned?"

Jesus stood up and, looking around, said to the scribes and
Pharisees, "He who is without sin among you, let him throw a stone
at her first."

With that proclamation, Jesus returned to writing on the ground.

The crowd of accusers drifted away until no one was left. Jesus
then stood again and asked the woman if there was anyone left to
condemn her. When the woman replied, "No," His response to her
echoes as a lesson to us all. "I don't condemn you either. Go and
sin no more."

I love this passage from John 8. It is one of hope and mercy,
grace and truth! Note that Jesus didn't condone her sin. He told her,
in fact, to stop sinning! However, He showed her grace and mercy
while also addressing those who would condemn her.

The accusations laid against her weren't wrong, but the heart
motive of her accusers was. Sadly, my motivations weren't always
pure when I confronted someone about their sin. You can also see a

poor demonstration of how to treat someone caught in sin when I wrote about my church's response to the unwed mother.

I think we struggle in the church with how to respond to those whose sin is glaringly obvious. We seem to forget Jesus died for them. His harshest words were for the religious people of the day. Pride and religiosity may be greater barriers to relationship with God than the things we tend to judge in our own minds.

Maybe we're afraid that by demonstrating grace and mercy we will seem weak on sin. Need that be so? Jesus spoke to the heart, not to the behavior. As demonstrated in the John 8 story, He told her to sin no more, but by His act of mercy, He also demonstrated love!

There is a wonderful passage of Scripture found in Matthew 7:1–5 (NKJV).

> Judge not, that you be not judged. For with what judgment you judge, you will be judged; and with the measure you use, it will be measured back to you. And why do you look at the speck in your brother's eye, but do not consider the plank in your own eye? Or how can you say to your brother, "Let me remove the speck from your eye"; and look, a plank is in your own eye? Hypocrite! First remove the plank from your own eye, and then you will see clearly to remove the speck from your brother's eye.

If we would remember that we ourselves have sinned and been forgiven much, we would find it easier to extend grace to others.

So the next time you feel the need to "help" someone by pointing out their offense, swallow your spiritual pride, check your heart, and show the love of Christ! I say this recognizing that there will be times when we need to speak truth in love, showing a brother or sister their need to repent. Most often though, people know when they are sinning, and our kind words and actions can help them find their way back onto the path of righteousness. As I mentioned before, restoration and redemption should be the end goal. Our desire should be that of seeing a brother or sister restored in their relationship with the King of Kings and Lord of Lords!

Taking It Deeper

1. Have you ever felt unsettled by change?

2. What does grace look like to you?

3. Have you ever experienced the loving correction of God?

4. Is there someone in your life right now that you need to reach out to? Maybe you spoke a word of correction in an ungodly way without thought or have shown a lack of mercy and understanding.

5. Meditate on Romans 8:1 as it would apply to your life and the lives of those around you.

Father, I pray for mercy and grace. It is easier to ask for mercy and grace for myself than it is to show mercy and grace to others. Help me to have a humble heart and to seek redemption and restoration in the lives of those around me. Give me Your perspective on the people I encounter throughout the day. In Jesus' name, amen.

CHAPTER 3

The High Life

The pastor stepped behind the pulpit as the time of worship drew to a close. He shouted, "Money cometh!" On cue, the congregation responded, "Money cometh to me!" I had seen this ritual repeated on my prior visits to this church. Each time the offering was collected, the same routine happened.

It wasn't the first time I'd been disturbed by the focus on money.

Money, or the lack thereof, has been an issue affecting the church for generations. Some churches place a huge emphasis on giving. Others are hypercritical of churches that bring in donations only to see the money go toward the pastor's salary and church electric bills.

I often wonder where the balance is.

*   *   *

Shortly before leaving CCC (formerly GCC), my siblings and I began attending another church on Wednesday nights. I experienced great times of worship and loved the pastor's messages, which seemed particularly insightful. The church met in a shopping plaza and it felt "cutting edge" to me. Everyone was friendly and seemed genuine in their love for God.

I began attending regularly after we departed CCC. I noticed this church had a youth group that focused on the Word. Those who attended seemed a bit more mature as well.

Youth ministry can be very challenging. I have heard stories of those who serve the youth and how some have felt they were just marking time before getting promoted to being a "real" pastor.

One also has to factor in the parents who force or "strongly encourage" their youth to attend. It often seems that youth groups are nothing more than spiritualized babysitting services. Parents think they're keeping their teens out of trouble by sending them to youth group. I, for one, can attest that that never works. If a teen is going to find trouble, they'll find it at youth group if they don't find it anywhere else.

Other times, the kids are committed to spiritual growth, but the church itself has other plans. In fact, one friend wrote to tell me of an experience just like that.

> Soon after returning home, my husband and I attended a local church. The leadership quickly signed us up for membership. They needed youth leaders and asked us if we would be interested in the position. Of course, there were warning signs right away, but ...
>
> We took a membership "course" and there were some red flags, but we brushed them off.
>
> My husband and I, along with another woman, led the youth. Two kids showed up the first night. But God built it from there. Gradually, the group expanded until we had a dozen or so regulars in addition to the ones who came inconsistently. They came, asked questions, and searched authentically for God. Lives were changed, for real. For good.
>
> Some of the kids didn't come to church. Some partied on the weekends. A few didn't even have

homes. The church leaders grumbled. What was worse is the church kids weren't coming. They had never come, had never intended to come. But the church grumbled. They didn't want to support a ministry for someone else's kids.

We had meetings. We talked about Jesus. The kids were eating it up! They were learning to study the Bible, with less and less direction from us! They were praying together! They were starting to tell their friends about Jesus.

We had a great year and even attended a youth conference. We really felt God had blessed this work and these kids. Some of the young people were starting to come out on Sunday mornings too. But they didn't feel welcome. And the truth is we didn't either. We started to feel more and more tension as these kids who just "didn't fit" started to come to Jesus and look for their place in the church.

As we wound down for the year and made plans for the following year, we asked our young people what they wanted for the next year. We did a little survey, asking them what they had learned, what they liked and didn't like, and what they'd like to see happen as we moved forward.

We had an overwhelming response, which made us so proud of these young people! Each and every one of them told us that they wanted to learn more about how to study the Bible themselves. Every one of them said they wanted to play fewer games; many wanted no game time at all. Most wanted to learn more and practice giving testimonies and telling their friends about their faith. They wanted to continue meeting with other young believers and worshipping together.

So we met with the church leadership to talk about the coming year. To this day, I feel sad when I think about that meeting. The elders and pastor agreed that they didn't want Bible study at youth group and they didn't care what the young people wanted. Nor did they care about the denomination's guidelines for youth ministry. They wanted the youth group run according to what they wanted for their children, who supposedly learned enough about God at home. They wanted youth group to be a fun place to come to "play games and stay out of trouble."

We were devastated. We pleaded the case for our kids, whose lives were changed by God Himself. We gave biblical examples, quoted the denomination's policy and statement of faith, and showed the surveys the kids had filled out.

The elders and pastor were not swayed. They didn't want the young people reading the Bible at church. They didn't want street people coming to church. They wanted a place where their children could come and play games, and they wanted us to provide it.

We had no choice but to step down. This was not something we could provide.

As we watched our young people fall away, confused and hurt, and look for acceptance elsewhere, we struggled with our own feelings of betrayal, rejection, and mistrust. We finally stopped attending when we felt like simply walking through the doors was participating in deceitfulness against God.

A short time later, the district administrator visited and closed the church.

Several months after all this happened, we were still hurt, confused and grieving, wondering what God's plan was for us and for the young people we had met, loved, and lost contact with.

One afternoon, we saw two of our girls fundraising at the local farmers market and, of course, stopped to talk with them. After a while, one of the girls pulled me aside and explained the reason behind their fundraising efforts.

"We're going to the youth conference," she explained. Not with another youth group, nor at the suggestion of a leader or parent. But they were still meeting together. They still talked about God, about their faith, about the things they did together as a youth group. They'd had such a great time at the youth conference we'd attended that they wanted to go again.

I think of "my girls," who are living for God now as wives and mothers ... I think of all the people they've been in contact with, knowing that they have a heart for God, a desire to share Jesus, and a knowledge of how to talk about their faith, to pray with each other, and to show love and respect to others. I wonder how many others they've touched ... I think of that and I'm certain that God is big enough to cover all of the ugliness and brokenness of His church, whom He loves in spite of it all. In spite of what we do and what we are. Because He is bigger than all of us and He has called us out and chosen us to be His people who love Him. And those girls, I'm sure they're better off ... And, well, that makes a little bit of hurting worthwhile.

—B. A.

Though some youth groups seem solid, I have also seen too much game playing in other youth groups. I often wonder why we don't challenge our youth. I'm not just talking about getting to know God's Word but about living it out as well. I would have thrived if I'd been given the opportunity to walk out my faith in a challenging way.

Just look at Joel 2:28.

> And it shall come to pass afterward, that I will pour out my Spirit on all flesh; your sons and your daughters shall prophesy, your old men shall dream dreams, and your young men shall see visions.

This is emphasized in Acts 2:17.

> And in the last days it shall be, God declares, that I will pour out my Spirit on all flesh, and your sons and your daughters shall prophesy, and your young men shall see visions, and your old men shall dream dreams.

Our youth aren't just kids. They are, right now, young men and women of God and should be encouraged to begin growing into that role.

I felt this was happening when I originally started attending my new youth group in the shopping plaza. The youth pastor really seemed to care for the kids who came. He would check in with us throughout the week, give rides, and always challenge us to go deeper with God.

Once a month, we would have pizza, and that was a nice addition to the times we spent in the Word.

It seemed like no time had passed before we went from one room at the plaza to three. The expansions were needed because the attendance was growing at a healthy clip. There finally came a day when the church moved to a bigger facility with multiple rooms, a kitchen, and a rather large sanctuary. Everyone was excited by the growth, but once we reached this new facility, things began to change.

I first noticed the changes in our youth meetings. Our pizza times were replaced with trips to the mall or to a water park. Not everyone in the youth group could afford these trips and the youth pastor would reach out to cover the costs. Twice, our youth group had the chance to go to a major Christian concert. Everyone in the youth group went. My siblings and I were unable to afford to go, and our youth pastor knew that. He kindly paid the way for us, but we knew we were there on his dime. We appreciated the gift but felt bad having to receive it.

Over time, the youth group also started moving from Bible studies to lighter programs during our youth meetings. It was a shift I wasn't keen on.

*   *   *

It was time for the church to make another move. This time, they wanted a facility that would be new and made to order, as opposed to using a facility that had once been something else.

The reasons for this move had nothing to do with attendance. Our current facility had ample room for the number of people attending and could have seated even more. As I listened to the plans for the church—plans that included a gym, recreation center, cooking facilities, and—oh yes—a church sanctuary, I became confused as to why this move was needed.

One day, after plans were solidified and the property purchased, the pastor made another announcement: they

> **Here's a Thought**
>
> Many churches offer budget coaching, cooking classes, and soup kitchens. That, to me, is love in action.
>
> "Little children, let us not love in word or talk but in deed and in truth" (1 John 3:18).

didn't want to build their own church before helping to build a church overseas on the mission field. In no time, the funds to build a facility in Africa were quickly donated.

I stayed with this church through part of the construction phase and then eased myself out. A period of poverty made attendance at this particular church out of my family's league.

* * *

Maybe it was the time, maybe the location, but I always seemed to find myself in a church that was filled with wealthy people or churches that wanted to "name and claim" the wealth!

When we moved to East Tennessee, my dad started his own business. Though my dad did his best, the times, the economy, and various other factors meant that the business did not perform as well as it could have. As a part of a family struggling with poverty, I was very discouraged when church members would mention sin as a reason for poverty. It seemed that after my dad's business struggled and we were buried under a bad economy and circumstances beyond our control, people began to point the finger.

I found out that, according to these helpful believers, our poverty was supposed to be temporary. We might receive help for a bill, but if we couldn't make the next payment, there must be sin in our life.

We would rack our brains trying to figure out what we had done wrong, what sin had been committed that would relegate us to poverty. It was disheartening and helped pave the road toward my frustration with "churchianity."

Once, a church reached out to provide groceries for our family. We were extremely excited and felt blessed beyond measure—until my mom opened the bags of food. Every item was out of date or severely dented and damaged. I'll never forget how much pain that caused my mom. In my current position, I oversee two food banks and I have my staff and volunteers ensure that every item we place in our food bags is in date, fresh, and dent free. Items past their expiration dates (even when the item is good for some time after) can give people the perception that they have received lower quality items.

Whether it is in our own poverty or that of others, we have the chance see Jesus. One story shared with me recently was of a life-changing encounter with the poor.

> It was love at first sight! That long, brown, wavy hair and those eyes that spoke louder than words could ever express. As I dared looking deep into the soul of another, I found the love of my life ... Jesus!
>
> It was in my introduction to Al (not his real name) that I realized that part of participating in God's kingdom meant our involvement with the special people who are on God's heart: the poor, needy, widowed, orphaned, and alien.
>
> It was on a cold Thursday evening in November 2005 when I first met Al. I came over, introduced myself, shook his hand, and asked him the everyday question "How are you?" The response was not your typical "Fine" or "Good." It was, "Well, things aren't going so great ..."
>
> What was I to do? Did I dare ask more leading questions? Did I brush him off and move on. I knew in that moment that Jesus wanted me to engage—engage with the need and the hurt of this man, engage with compassion and love like Jesus so often modeled in the Gospels.
>
> Al went on to share his story with me about being on the street in the summer with his two children (nine and eleven at the time). They had just recently got into a public housing unit in the fall but had no money and no income, and the city was going to cut off their heat because of overdue bills.

That's when I knew ministry was going to look a lot different to me from what I had been used to in the past. I had been used to training teams, running programs, and leading schools for Christians who wanted to take adventurous steps in their faith. Though that has an important place to play, my life in ministry was starting to be defined by loving the poor and becoming friends with the marginalized of society. Our society. All societies.

Since 2005, Al and I have actually become really good friends! Our relationship is no longer defined by me helping him because he's the needy one and I'm the giver. We truly have a relationship that we define together in friendship. I've been involved in things in his life, as he has been involved in mine.

I have discovered that ministry to the poor, needy, orphaned, widowed, or alien isn't just about a one-shot handout or a random act of kindness; it's about discovering friendship and realizing each other's needs and the need for Jesus in our lives! I'm becoming more convinced that the best container for the kingdom of God to be manifested through is friendships. I look in John 15, and one of Jesus' last words to His disciples is that He calls them His friends, which somehow graduated them from His servants. Interesting!

Read John 15:12–15 (NIV).

My command is this: Love each other as I have loved you. Greater love has no one than this, that he lay down his life for his friends. You are my friends if you do what I command. I no longer call you servants, because a servant does not know his

master's business. Instead, I have called you friends,
for everything that I learned from my Father I have
made known to you.

—D. N.

*   *   *

The Bible says not to hold the wealthy in higher regard than
those who are poor.

> My brothers, show no partiality as you hold the
> faith in our Lord Jesus Christ, the Lord of glory.
> For if a man wearing a gold ring and fine clothing
> comes into your assembly, and a poor man in shabby
> clothing also comes in, and if you pay attention to
> the one who wears the fine clothing and say, "You
> sit here in a good place," while you say to the poor
> man, "You stand over there," or, "Sit down at my
> feet," have you not then made distinctions among
> yourselves and become judges with evil thoughts?
> —James 2:1–4

My wife, Sarah, and I recall a time when we saw this take place
in a public meeting. We were attending a small country church that
had members steeped in poverty. However, when a wealthy friend
of the pastor showed up, people nearly fell over themselves making
her feel welcomed and would gravitate toward her, hovering to be a
part of whatever conversation she was involved in. She was publicly
acknowledged from the pulpit and thanked for coming.

On the opposite side of the coin, however, while my wife and
I were serving as missionaries in Croatia, we were blessed by the
love and presence of others. We had very low support levels and
many times barely scraped by. Leon was part of the US military
peacekeeping presence in Croatia after the war. We connected at a

church service and Leon never once blinked at the fact that my wife and I didn't have much to work with financially on the mission field. He would eat with us, invite us to his house for dinner, walk with us, take us out for meals, come to church, participate in ministry, and gift us with some of the best iced tea imaginable on a very regular basis. He showed love and spoke compassion through his presence!

Sylvie was another woman whose job with the American government brought her to Croatia, and who ministered to us through her actions. She spent time taking us for meals, coming to our home, and involving herself in our work with the orphanages. She was friendly and sweet, and when she returned to the United States, she left everything she couldn't take back with her for missionaries and Croats who couldn't otherwise afford these items. These were just a couple of the friends we made who chose to demonstrate humility and walk in gratitude for the blessings God had given them.

I realize now that, due to my experiences with poverty, I just wasn't comfortable in a church that put a heightened emphasis on wealth. Add to these experiences the fact that I had already been burned by what I felt was an abusive church and had been hurt by those in authority. You may understand why, at times, I felt as if I wanted to run away. However, God wasn't done with me yet.

*   *   *

Hopefully by now you can see areas where the church needs to wake up. Areas like church discipline, poverty, and authority have been abused and mishandled over the years by many churches. However, I don't think we need to throw the proverbial baby out with the bathwater.

I didn't see it at the time, but my identity as a believer was being shaped by these experiences. Later, we'll look at how these three areas affected one another.

What I Learned on the Way to the Resurrection

3. Poverty is not a sin. Neither is being rich.

I believe we Christians need a reality check when it comes to poverty and wealth. I have seen many books written with the goal of encouraging Christians to reach out to the poor around us.

The basic premise usually includes lots of statistics about the dispersing of wealth to those in needy countries, citing endless Scriptures about helping the poor, the widows, and the orphans. These are valid Scriptures and I believe all Christians should be encouraged to reach out to the world around them. However, I believe the result of many of these pleas is guilt and frustration. Many Christians feel guilty that they don't have enough money to help or feel condemned for not doing enough. Others feel that those in poverty have brought it on themselves.

I believe Jesus absolutely wants us to help those in need. We should all look for ways to help those less fortunate, but if our motive is to relieve guilt, we're better off saving our money.

The question may go to how you see poverty and wealth. If you see poverty as a sin, then your desire to help may not be there. Granted, some people do make bad choices which result in the loss of income. There are those who misuse available funds by buying alcohol and other substances and then find themselves in dire straits. However, there are many more people around the world suffering from involuntary poverty than those we see with self-inflicted wounds. Sickness, layoffs, and geographic location can all contribute to a lack of financial stability. Most often, it just takes one or two missed paychecks to send people on a downward spiral. The Bible specifically tells us not to mock the poor (Proverbs 17:5), not to oppress those in poverty (Proverbs 14:31), and not to turn a deaf ear to their cries (Proverbs 21:13)!

One often cited Scripture is found in the Beatitudes, where Jesus starts off His message with the opening statement "Blessed are you poor, for yours is the kingdom of God" (Luke 6:20, NKJV). I look at that Scripture and see an example of our heart attitude. When we are unencumbered with the cares of life, when we have fewer material distractions, it is easier to focus on the King of Kings. When our own resources aren't enough, we can draw from Christ's resources. Those in poverty can give other things besides their money. They can give of themselves: their time, their presence, and their availability can bless those in need.

I remember one particular lady in Zagreb, Croatia. Baka (Grandmother) Maria was a dear, elderly woman who was a Bosnian refugee forced to flee during the Balkan Wars. She had no money, scant possessions, and few items of clothing. What she had in abundance was love! After meeting Christ, she showed His transforming power by coming to her church every day to bake goodies for the staff and make lunch for any stranger who walked in the door. She was always ready with a hug and a smile, though she had known great losses: family, friends, belongings, and security, to name a few. She impacted more people with the living gospel than many who go out into the streets preaching the Word!

Regardless of how people end up in these situations, we are called to help. In the New Testament, we see references to selling our belongings and helping the poor. James says,

> Religion that God our Father accepts as pure and faultless is this: to look after orphans and widows in their distress and to keep oneself from being polluted by the world.
> —James 1:27 (NIV)

Does it seem at times like a losing battle? Absolutely. However, God didn't release us from the fight. Poverty isn't a sin; doing nothing is!

With that in mind, we should remember that wealth is not a sin either. We are told that the love of money is the root of evil, but we are not discouraged from acquiring wealth. In fact, scriptural examples of those with wealth show that believers used those funds to glorify God. From Abraham in the Old Testament to the early church in Acts, Christians exemplified their love for God and others by distributing their funds to those in need.

Having money is just another opportunity God has given us to bless those in need. I believe that whether you are poor or rich, you should love the Lord God with all your heart, soul, mind, and strength and love your neighbor as yourself (Luke 10:27)! If every child of God did that, regardless of their financial standing, the church would be a lot stronger today!

Taking It Deeper

1. How has your economic situation impacted your view of God and others?

2. Setting aside your current economic state, can you list at least three things you are thankful for?

3. What is one way you can show love for those around you that does not involve money?

4. Is there a local thrift store or food bank in your town? How can you get involved?

5. Spend some time praying for those in a different financial situation than your own.

Father, You know what state my finances are in. Please help this situation not to become a distraction from reaching out to others around me. Let me be rich in love, mercy, and friendship in whatever sphere of influence I am in. In Jesus' name, amen.

CHAPTER 4

The Ol' Country Church

I have read numerous books over the last couple years that look at the topic of Christianity from a "freedom from religion" type of approach. The idea is legalism (i.e., religion) is bad and there's freedom in Christ! In many ways, I respond well to the antireligious mind-set. I believe Christ came so that we could have life! John 10:10 says, "The thief comes only to steal and kill and destroy. I came that they may have life and have it abundantly."

In one sense, I found my joy diminishing when I moved from bad church experience to bad church experience. My faith seemed like it was on life support. I was allowing circumstances to affect my walk with God. I would enter a church and look for the negative. I felt that even a hint of legalism was enough to abandon ship, so to speak.

Another struggle was my ongoing desire to maintain a good public face as an on-fire, strong child of God. Inside, I was dying spiritually! I desired freedom from religion. I felt like damaged goods and worshipping the Lord in freedom appealed to me more and more! I felt like I was drowning and my desire was to find a place where I could be free to worship God without religion!

The danger is that those discovering new freedom from a religious mind-set sometimes go to the opposite extreme and take an "anything goes" approach to faith.

* * *

As the music played, people began to lift their hands into the air and worship the Lord. I stood among the crowd, at an aisle seat, with my eyes closed and my arms stretched out in praise. I was somewhat startled when I felt someone smack my hand. I attempted to ignore the distraction. My hand was bumped a second time and then my head and shoulders were tapped as well. I opened my eyes to see a lady in the church jumping up and down, twitching, dancing, and waving her arms all around. She bumped her way up the aisle and, when she reached the front of the church, she fell to the ground.

Her dress had flown up over her head.

As if on cue, an elderly lady in the church quietly moved to the front and covered the lady's body with a blanket until she was ready to stand back up.

For some reason, I came back to this church a couple of more times, but the experience of being jostled during worship happened again and again. I didn't feel comfortable in that setting.

I look back and find it funny now, but at the time, it was confusing and frightening. I was just leaving my teens and what I was seeing in this church during the worship time just made me feel too uneasy. Everyone seemed to accept this as normal and

---

Dance Like Nobody's Watching!

I'm not opposed to people dancing, getting on their knees, or moving in general when worshipping the Lord.

I know 2 Samuel 6:14 is often cited, in which David danced before the Lord.

If you want to worship in movement, by all means do so. I don't think your worship should be a distraction to others though! Nowhere does it say David wildly bumped into other worshippers while praising the Lord!

no one addressed, at least publicly, the distraction or indecency of the actions.

*   *   *

While living in Tennessee, I would occasionally see news broadcasts about snake-handling churches. This bizarre ritual is based on a misinterpretation of a couple of passages of Scripture. The first is found in Acts 28:1–6 where Paul was bitten by a snake.

> Once safely on shore, we found out that the island was called Malta. The islanders showed us unusual kindness. They built a fire and welcomed us all because it was raining and cold. Paul gathered a pile of brushwood and, as he put it on the fire, a viper, driven out by the heat, fastened itself on his hand. When the islanders saw the snake hanging from his hand, they said to each other, "This man must be a murderer; for though he escaped from the sea, the goddess Justice has not allowed him to live." But Paul shook the snake off into the fire and suffered no ill effects. The people expected him to swell up or suddenly fall dead; but after waiting a long time and seeing nothing unusual happen to him, they changed their minds and said he was a god.

The second passage used to justify snake handling is Luke 10:19. "I have given you authority to trample on snakes and scorpions and to overcome all the power of the enemy; nothing will harm you."

The abusive use of these Scriptures has led to many a death. Those deaths are interpreted as a lack of faith, which allowed the handler to be bitten and die. I had a fear that I would wander into a small country church one day and then they would lock the doors.

And bring out the snakes.

Which would bite me.

And I would die!

Thankfully, that never happened.

I did notice a few quirky things though. Like the people who would come to services with cans or cups in their hands. I soon found that this was so they had something to spit their chewing tobacco juice into during the service. Tobacco usage seemed to be widespread in these small country churches.

Many of the churches also had men and a few women standing around outside the front door. These folks would be busy making an extremely dense cloud of secondhand smoke for people to walk through on the way inside. Once inside, you would hear the occasional sermon condemning various vices like alcohol and tobacco. After the amen and the prayers, the cloud would return.

*   *   *

There was an old episode of *The Waltons* that I remember vividly. *The Waltons* was a show on network television in the United States from 1972 until 1981. It was a show about a Depression-era family growing up in Virginia. One episode in the first season was called "The Sinner." In this episode, a fire-and-brimstone preacher was practicing for a sermon in the yard and started screaming, "Repent!" As he got louder and louder, he began addressing sin and working himself into quite a frenzy. He began focusing on the people around him as he screamed, frightening the children.

I saw this happen more than once over the years. I remember one pastor getting so worked up that he began to slip into a rhythm. Every word was shouted out. *"Jesus-uh! He wants-uh you-uh to repent-uh!"* As he shouted these words, his face began to turn a dark, crimson red. I was afraid he would have an aneurism right there in the middle of the service. People were shouting amen and hallelujah left and right. Out would come his handkerchief to mop the sweat from his face. He would lean forward and shout. He somehow made it through the service without dying, but I never felt comfortable in these situations. I could never imagine Jesus shouting and turning tomato red while speaking to the crowds. I believe that people were drawn to Christ because of His humility, the truth that He spoke, and because He showed genuine love and compassion. Remember how the children wanted to come to Jesus as well. I can't imagine them doing that if He was yelling and screaming.

I'm not sure why it happens, but I saw quite a few of these fire-and-brimstone preachers shouting their messages. It seemed as if they thought the louder they shouted, the more impact their words would have.

*   *   *

I started attending one particular small country church which was nestled down by a creek bed. I soon found myself getting a bit more involved. The people seemed friendly, and it wasn't too long before the pastor asked me to preach.

I was encouraged that he allowed me the opportunity and that he was so forgiving when my first sermon was shorter than expected, due to my nervous speed-reading through the pages I had written. I had worked for a solid week on that message and used every resource I could find to add depth and insight into the passage of Scripture I wanted to expound on. In my excitement, I had written out the entire message word for word. I had timed myself and felt the message was long enough, but once I nervously delivered it, I probably clocked in around ten minutes. Undeterred, the pastor asked me to preach on numerous occasions and at one point asked me to be the youth pastor, a position I accepted. His early encouragement when I started out in ministry was a blessing.

One of the things I noticed about this and many of these country churches was that a lot of the people were illiterate. Even the pastor of this particular church was unable to read. He listened to the Bible on tape in order to get his messages. Many of the people would sit and listen to the messages but never open their Bibles or take notes. I was always concerned that their inability to read would mean that anyone could preach a false doctrine and they would never know. I believe the ability to read is a gift from God which we often ignore. Looking back now, I wish that our church had offered a literacy program as a part of its ministry

As much as I enjoyed this church, there came a day when sin "entered the camp" via the worship leader. When it was brought to my attention, I immediately went to the pastor to see how we would deal with it. The pastor didn't want to address the sin and I felt that we should ask the worship leader to step down. The church was slowly growing and the pastor felt that if the worship leader stepped down, it would affect attendance and membership. The worship leader was quite talented and the thought was expressed that he was not someone easily replaced.

From the depths of my heart, I felt this was the wrong approach. In fact, I felt the Lord urging me to speak a prophetic word at that point. This had never happened to me before. I felt that I must share these words with the pastor or I would be in disobedience. The word I felt led to share was "If this is dealt with in the right manner, the church will blossom. If it is not dealt with correctly, the church will close." The pastor didn't listen to this word and chose not to deal with the situation. Two weeks later, the church closed its doors forever.

I was scared by the pastor's refusal to address the issue, but even more scared that the church had closed. I was twenty years old and had never experienced a "word from the Lord" before.

*   *   *

My wife and I moved back to Tennessee after our wedding. I had to work one Sunday but suggested that my wife visit a church one of my friends attended. She was supposed to take a left when getting off the interstate. Instead, she accidentally took a right and found a small church getting ready to start. She enjoyed the service and for a while we went to this church every Sunday.

The music was mostly hymns and the messages fairly solid. As a body, the people got together for fellowship and dinners outside the church setting. It was very enjoyable. The people seemed to care for one another and we had lots of fun times with amazing conversations about life and the Lord.

The pastor worked part-time as a life insurance agent. The church was small enough that he couldn't make ends meet on what he was being paid. One Sunday, the pastor announced that he was stepping down and would be selling life insurance on a full-time basis.

His replacement seemed like a nice enough fellow, but people began to leave soon after he took over.

It started one Sunday in the spring. It was an election year and the Republicans and Democrats were in their primary season, a time when a bunch of candidates get whittled down to two who will oppose each other in the November presidential election. On this particular Sunday, our bulletins included an insert with all the Republican candidates and their stances on moral and political issues that many Christians are concerned about. There was no corresponding sheet for the Democratic candidates. I mentioned that to my wife and shortly after that, an older couple opened their bulletin and the gentleman began raising his voice and saying how he wouldn't be told how to vote. He felt that by only including one party, the church was saying if you're a Christian, you had to vote a certain way. I did not disagree with his assumption. I have noticed over the years that when it comes to politics, Jesus is usually equated with one party. This couple would not stand for it so they got up and left, never to return.

Another Sunday, the pastor began introducing praise and worship choruses to our services. That was too much for some at this small church and more people left. It was only a matter of time before the doors eventually closed for good.

*   *   *

From extreme forms of the charismatic movement to the ultra-legalistic conservative church, I saw all sides of the coin at these small churches and never felt comfortable for long in any one of them.

Shortly before returning to the mission field, my wife and I were asked to share at one country church that seemed to be growing with God. After I shared, I received a phone call asking me if I'd be interested in becoming the pastor of this congregation. Explaining our imminent return to the field, I politely declined. A year and a half later, when we returned from Croatia, I was again asked to step in, this time as co-pastor. I accepted, though the church was vastly different than when we had left.

Apparently, the church had split on the issue of homosexuality. A member of the church had "suspected" a couple of members were involved in this lifestyle and wanted the pastor not only to preach against the sin but also to name those in the church he felt lived this lifestyle.

When the pastor refused to do such a thing, the member began a campaign of gossip, informing members of the community that this church endorsed the sin of homosexuality. He left and took many members with him. We arrived to see a shell of the former church. This pastor was hurt by all that had happened and asked me if I was comfortable coleading a church that had gained this reputation. I was at a point in my life, having just turned thirty, where I was embracing the antireligion mind-set. I felt, and still do, that all we could do was speak biblical truth and let God be the judge. We could speak to sin and let the Holy Spirit convict those who needed to turn from a path of unrighteousness. I did not believe in public shaming for those trapped in sin. I myself was not without sin and not ready to cast stones.

Into this congregation, my wife and I poured our time and energy. We shared messages that came out of our missions experience and wrote a basic discipleship course which we took the congregation through. We have continued to develop and use that course over the years.

The church building had been for sale for some time, but the owner had promised we wouldn't be kicked out. We were supposed to have advance notice of any impending sales. However, one Friday I received a phone call that the church had sold and we needed to be out before Sunday. Scrambling, we removed our belongings and phoned all the members with the news. Not having a plan in place, we asked everyone to come to our house on Sunday where we would pray, worship, and plan.

As you will see in the next chapter, this was not my first experience with house churches.

What I Learned on the Way to the Resurrection

4. You are never too young, too old, too uneducated, too poor, or too busy to serve the Lord!

I was the missions director of my church at fifteen. I wasn't much older than twenty when I was asked to be a youth pastor. When I was twenty-one, I traveled with an itinerant evangelist in his late seventies. I couldn't keep up with his energy!

It is a sad but true fact that over the years the church has relegated the young and the aged to the pews and youth groups. I've heard numerous stories of people who were told that they needed to be older in order to serve God. I have also seen the elderly members of a church ignored when it came to ministry opportunities.

> And let us not grow weary of doing good, for in due season we will reap, if we do not give up. So then, as we have opportunity, let us do good to everyone, and especially to those who are of the household of faith.
>
> —Galatians 6:9–10

How can we do good? By serving and loving others and by sharing the truth of Jesus Christ. For that job description, age doesn't matter.

You may recall this passage of Scripture:

> And in the last days it shall be, God declares, that I will pour out my Spirit on all flesh, and your sons and your daughters shall prophesy, and your young men shall see visions, and your old men shall dream dreams.
>
> —Acts 2:17

I like the following passage, found in Joshua 14. Caleb is telling part of his story to Joshua and the Israelites when he says,

> And now, behold, the Lord has kept me alive, just as he said, these forty-five years since the time that the Lord spoke this word to Moses, while Israel walked in the wilderness. And now, behold, I am this day eighty-five years old. I am still as strong today as I was in the day that Moses sent me; my strength now is as my strength was then, for war and for going and coming. So now give me this hill country of which the Lord spoke on that day, for you heard on that day how the Anakim were there, with great fortified cities. It may be that the Lord will be with me, and I shall drive them out just as the Lord said.
>
> —Joshua 14:10–12

He was eighty-five years old and still ready to go for God! However, the youth can also be mightily used by God! Remember Samuel the prophet was called by God as a youth. The Bible talks of two kings: Joash, who assumed the throne at the age of seven, and Josiah, who became king at the age of eight. The Bible says that both of them obeyed the Lord (2 Kings 12:2, 22:2).

Our young people are a valuable resource and many of them have a drive and initiative to do something! Look at how many projects have been launched by young people. They want to change the world. What better way to change the world than to encourage and help them do it through the church, with solid discipleship? Youth are turning away from the church today. We need to give them a reason to stay.

Our older generations are an untapped resource as well. Retirement does not mean they stop living or have given up on their hopes and dreams. We can and should learn much from our elders. Why not partner the energy of our youth with the wisdom of our elders? Imagine what advancements we could see for the kingdom of God then!

Nor do you need to be educated to serve God. True biblical education happens when you leave the Bible college or missionary training school. It happens just like it did for the apostles, when you rub up against the world. In the military, every battle plan gets changed upon first contact with the enemy. The same holds true for life. We may come away from seminary or missions training school with vast amounts of knowledge, but that doesn't always help when you meet real suffering. Faith becomes real when you talk to victims of war, family members devastated by suicide, and someone who has just lost their job! Remember that Peter and a few of the other disciples were just plain old uneducated fishermen. Yet God used these uneducated men to change the world!

I'm not knocking education, but education, or the lack thereof, is no excuse to sit idly by the sidelines and hope others will share the love of Jesus Christ. Any person at any age can and should do that. The Great Commission is for all of us!

Taking It Deeper

1. What are some things you have experienced in church that have caused you confusion or made you unsettled in some way?

2. Do you feel that God is able to use you in service to Him right now?

3. What, in your opinion, may be lacking in your ability to share the gospel in word or deed?

4. Take some time and look at the life of Peter in the four Gospels and then in Acts. What do you think contributed to his change from fisherman to church leader? How can you apply that to your own life?

5. Who can you seek out in your church to "partner with" in serving others?

Father, I do not always feel adequate enough to serve You. I feel that I lack in some areas and that I might mess up in my efforts to advance the kingdom. I am also a little scared. Help me to boldly seek out others in my church to walk with in service to You. Allow me to expand my circle of friends to include young and old alike. In Jesus' name, amen.

CHAPTER 5

Home

And they devoted themselves to the apostles'
teaching and the fellowship, to the breaking of
bread and the prayers. And awe came upon every
soul, and many wonders and signs were being done
through the apostles. And all who believed were
together and had all things in common. And they
were selling their possessions and belongings and
distributing the proceeds to all, as any had need.
And day by day, attending the temple together and
breaking bread in their homes, they received their
food with glad and generous hearts, praising God
and having favor with all the people. And the Lord
added to their number day by day those who were
being saved.

—Acts 2:42–47

This Scripture seems to be the one most often cited by those
involved in the house church movement.

There are many variations on the house church model, but the
common theme seems to be the free and easy sharing of the Word
of God. Everyone is encouraged to participate and have a voice.

Sometimes, there is no leader or the leadership role is minimized. There may be food and beverages served in order to make people feel more relaxed and at ease with one another. The social aspect of house church seems to be at the very core of why people participate. Often cited is the sense of community.

The idea of having church in a home was appealing to me on many levels. The main thing for me was that the setting would allow, in theory, for a more relaxed atmosphere. It didn't always work out that way, hence the "in theory" part.

I remember my first encounter with a house church. My family, along with a few others, had left CCC and was now gathering in our home for a time of worship and Bible study. I was still involved with a youth group at another church but thought the idea of staying home and having church sounded like fun.

The house church itself started off well. We had very interesting Bible studies and the worship times were filled with songs we had all come to know and love at CCC. We were all encouraged to go deeper with God. One of the teens was preparing to leave for a five-month Youth With A Mission DTS (Discipleship Training School). I was able to save my money from working all summer, which

> ### Everybody Is Somebody
>
> I believe every believer has something to offer.
>
> "What is the outcome then, brethren? When you assemble, each one has a psalm, has a teaching, has a revelation, has a tongue, has an interpretation. Let all things be done for edification" (1 Corinthians 14:26, NASB).
>
> This isn't restricted to just the house church setting. It can happen in traditional church settings as well. I believe that God has given each of us talents that can add depth to any church service.

allowed me to spend a week in California volunteering at the US Center for World Missions. I had first learned of the USCWM a couple years earlier. After sending away for a map, I was put into contact with one of the staff there. I began a communication with the staff member, and the result was that at age seventeen, I was about to begin my first real adventure in missions.

At the house church, we would share meals and some of us would toss the football out in the side yard after service. Things moved along well for a while. After a season, there began to be some disunity in our group over who would lead worship. Instead of working together, division over who should lead popped up. It began to cause some friction and no one was quite sure how to address the situation.

After a time, other issues began to emerge as well. Personal opinions and feelings began to creep into our conversations. Thoughts on relationships and whether one should marry or not became quite divisive. Sometimes, it seemed like these issues became all that we talked about. I know that we had some great biblical discussions, but the underlying tension became palpable at times.

This issue was not the entire cause of the church dissolution but was a contributing factor. Feelings were hurt and a once close-knit group dissolved before my eyes.

Though this first experience with a home group didn't work out, I still found the concept appealing.

*   *   *

One day I opened the newspaper and saw an advertisement for a new house church meeting in another town. Touted as being modeled on the book of Acts, the "Open Church" sounded interesting and my mom and I thought we would drive out and check into it.

The initial group we encountered was rather large and all the chairs were arrayed in a circle. They talked about the structure of the group and then the group began discussing the Bible.

I enjoyed myself until one fellow began to espouse beliefs that even I, as a Christian of just a few years, recognized as not biblically accurate. My knowledge of the Bible wasn't enough to refute his points though, so I remained silent and waited for the leadership to speak up and point this fellow back to the right path.

I waited.

Nothing happened.

No one ever spoke up and corrected him as he continued sharing what I knew to be wrong biblical interpretations of the Word.

No one wanted to be seen as a taking charge, and therefore there was no leader, which meant "anything goes" was the norm. The entire evening felt very unsettling. As I drove home with my mom, we discussed the man who brought this interpretation of the Word and how we both felt someone should have spoken up. We didn't visit this house church a second time.

It was a long time before I became involved in house churches again. This was simply because I didn't encounter anyone running a house church in my locale. I wasn't opposed to the idea, if done correctly. Sadly, for every good house church experience—and I know many people who have really enjoyed and been blessed by house churches—there are also those negative experiences which could really hurt someone.

That was what nearly happened to K. M., as you will see in the story she shared with me.

> I was so excited because it (the house church) reminded me of the early church: we ate together, prayed together, and fellowshipped together. We were tight and it was all good from what I could see. I left for a five-month YWAM DTS and when I came back home, I noticed a lot of tension going on and some people leaving. Instead of getting involved with all the muck, I took off for my next mission trip, which lasted for two years.
>
> Coming back, our church supported another girl and me to do some intercity missions. I knew it wasn't where I was supposed to be and decided

to return home instead. I was offered a room in the pastor's house up the side of a mountain so he could "disciple" me. I didn't have any good feelings about that. I felt that if I moved to that mountain, I would get stuck up there somehow.

The pastor told me and others about how my roommate was messing up her life and in rebellion to the ministry. I believed some of what they said. They made me feel on the "in." I was just glad they weren't talking about me. In church, they would call out people's iniquities and embarrass them in front of everyone. They did this to my friend and hurt her terribly. I started to see that something was very wrong. She stopped going up to the house church on Sundays.

Let me just interrupt this story for a moment to say that this is church abuse at its worst. While in my previous story it was a lack of leadership which caused problems, here you see the danger of a controlling and manipulative leader. Back to K. M's story.

Everyone was worried about Y2K and started to stockpile canned food and guns. There was talk about the end times and how the government might come against us. People took out second mortgages on their homes to give to the pastor so his family could have a privileged lifestyle. High school graduates were "discipled" at the pastor's place. They lived in little cabins that were on the property. Other people moved up the mountain, got property, or settled on the pastor's land.

The pastor said a whole bunch of garbage, such as that demons lived in the rafters of churches and that we didn't dare step into the churches again or demons might get on us. There was a lot of manipulation and control in the "family church."

When I realized there was something terribly wrong, I burned my bridges and confronted the pastor, through a letter, about where things were wrong. I prayed that this church would die because it was a cult and very bad. Slowly, it did. The pastor and his wife divorced and everyone left, some faster than others. Unfortunately, I've heard that the "pastor" is still up to no good and starting things up again in a new part of town—same ol' thing with a new wife and new followers.

Fortunately for us, the believers who were there are all in new churches, spread out, and are useful vessels for God.

—K. M.

According to K. M., those who participated in and had been hurt by this house church were eventually renewed, healed, and restored—except for the head pastor, who chose to continue down the wrong path. I praise God that the people involved in this story were able to understand that they had been led astray and hurt by a person, not by the living God. Because things are done in His name, people who are victimized blame not only the one perpetuating the abuse but also God Himself.

I believe God weeps over our pain and wants to heal our brokenness. As it says in Psalm 147:3, "He heals the brokenhearted and binds up their wounds."

*   *   *

I was on the mission field and struggling with numerous personal issues when I next encountered the house church. I found myself becoming frustrated with organized religion and felt that I wasn't experiencing life the way it was meant to be.

Another missionary took me under his wing and began to explain his involvement in the house church movement. He made a statement that resonated with where I was. He said, "If you go to a movie theater, you'll notice everyone looking at the front, watching a show. No interaction, just seeing the backs of people's heads and watching what happens. Now go to a church and you'll notice the same thing. Church is like a movie theater."

Boom!

It was as if a bomb had gone off in my mind.

Finally, after all these years, someone hit the nail on the head. Someone understood what I was feeling. Church seemed way too stuffy, organized, and religious. I needed "life" and believed I wasn't going to find it in the four walls of a church building.

My righteous indignation kicked in and I was now looking for faults in every church I visited. My friend began to loan me a few of his house church/cell church books. The more books I read on the topic, the more irritated I became with churchianity. I wanted to turn away from that type of structure. This was hard to do on the mission field, as we needed to be involved with the local communities. I began working myself up to the point where I felt as if I were suffocating alive inside a "dead, lifeless" church. I wanted freedom. I convinced myself that the freedom I was looking for could only be found in the house church.

We began visiting our friend's cell church, in addition to the other churches in the community. People were laughing, friendly, and open to what God had for them. We visited a few times but knew that this was our friend's mission work and didn't want to take away from it or interfere with it. We only visited a few times, but coupled with the material he fed me, I wanted to experience church the way it was "meant to be."

In my "righteousness," I began to tell others how the way the church was doing it was wrong. I was sure I knew a better way. Now I just needed opportunity.

I believe now that God, in His mercy, kept me from foolishly launching into something I truly knew nothing about. I was motivated by frustration and hurt, not by biblical love and compassion. The material I read was not the problem, rather my interpretation of it. I was operating out of my own pain and, but for the grace of God, could have caused much harm and damage to the body of Christ.

A few years passed before I was to experience house churches again.

*   *   *

Back at home, after this overseas venture, our church building had sold and we gathered the people from the congregation in our home.

We asked what the congregation wanted to do and most seemed content to continue meeting at our place. We thought we would try it out for a short season, with the intent of seeing people move on to other churches as they felt comfortable. The church building being sold so quickly caught everyone by surprise, and we figured that after a period of adjustment, most would move on and find a new place to worship.

So began another adventure.

My wife, Sarah, led worship every week and I prepared most of the messages. Our meetings were casual, since we were in our own home. We still gathered tithes and offerings, which were then split between buying supplies for the house church and sending donations to missionaries overseas. Our financial books were open to everyone in the church. In fact, they were literally open beside the offering basket. People trusted us and we kept a detailed ledger as to income received and dispersed.

After we'd been meeting together for a while, the majority of the people was now getting involved in churches somewhere else. We lived in a trailer park at the time and my daughter's friends would see cars coming down to our house every Sunday morning. Before too long, various kids began to show up at our door. We were thinking that the time had come to close our house church adventure when, to our surprise, even more kids began to show up. Sarah talked with their parents to let them know we were having church and the parents agreed to let their kids come down on Sunday mornings.

I wasn't sure how I felt about this. I wasn't really into leading a children's church, but that was what it became. Every Sunday we would have a group of kids show up and my wife and I led them in interactive kids songs. A few of the kids decided they wanted to help lead the singing, even writing their own songs, which contained themes they were learning on Sundays, and their styling came from whatever popular music was playing on their parents' radios at the time. It was fun to see their excitement and enthusiasm and to know we were providing a place where they could feel safe. Some adults from the previous church family continued to attend as they were able, providing food for shared lunches and sowing into the children's lives.

I began to tell Bible stories, and over the next year, we made sure every kid had a Bible they could understand. We talked about the simple lessons children could learn from Scripture and I always made time for the kids to ask any questions they wanted about God.

My heart was blessed when my daughter and a neighbor girl both wanted to receive Jesus Christ as Savior. It became the highlight of our time together.

There came a day when we decided to move across town. It meant we had to shut down the kids' church, but we felt it was time. We said our good-byes and moved away.

* * *

I was still dying on the inside. Though blessed by the "good things" that had happened, I felt like someone would find out I was faking. I still believed in God; it just felt like my outward display of "Christianity" was an act, because it was in conflict with my home life and inner thought life. I found myself doubting God's faithfulness, His love, and His compassion. Some of this was due to sin I was struggling with in my own life. Some was due to all the disappointment I had been experiencing in my faith walk and experience with Christianity. It all tied together to make me a miserable individual.

What I Learned on the Way to the Resurrection

5. Effective and godly leaders are those who live lives fully surrendered to Jesus Christ.

Leaders can inspire people to greatness, but they can also be abusive and condescending. Effective leadership can change the world, and ineffective leadership can destroy lives.

Despite what I have seen and experienced in some house churches, leadership is not a negative thing. God Himself appointed leaders throughout the Old Testament. Moses was called by God to lead the people out of bondage. Exodus 3:10 says, "So now, go. I am sending you to Pharaoh to bring my people the Israelites out of Egypt." And Joshua led the people into the Promised Land. (See the book of Joshua.) Joshua was told by the Lord what his job was in Deuteronomy 31:23. "The LORD gave this command to Joshua son of Nun: 'Be strong and courageous, for you will bring the Israelites into the land I promised them on oath, and I myself will be with you.'"

In Matthew 28:20, Jesus called the apostles to teach the church all that He had taught them after He ascended into heaven.

Look at this passage in Ephesians:

> And He gave some as apostles, and some as prophets, and some as evangelists, and some as pastors and teachers, for the equipping of the saints for the work of service, to the building up of the body of Christ.
> —Ephesians 4:11–12 (NASB)

Guess what. Those are all positions of leadership.

We need not be afraid of leadership; we should instead encourage our leaders to be godly men and women! In fact, we should do more than encourage them. We should be praying for them as well.

"I urge, then, first of all, that petitions, prayers, intercession, and thanksgiving be made for all people— for kings and all those in authority, that we may live peaceful and quiet lives in all godliness and holiness" (1 Timothy 2:1–2).

How often do we pray for our pastors, elders, deacons, etc.? Do we encourage those who bring the Word of the Lord to us? I believe that if we prayed more for our leaders, we would have leaders that are more effective.

The Bible also gives us amazing models of godly leadership, and the best model of leadership I have found in the Word of God is Jesus Christ Himself.

Jesus Christ modeled servant leadership. Even with all His authority, He still walked in humility. He said that the disciples would do even greater things than He did (John 14:12). Of course, the best example of His leadership was when He, the Son of God, got down on His hands and knees and washed the disciples' feet! All the dirt and grime from travel, He washed with His own hands. Not only did He wash the feet of those who loved Him, He washed the feet of the one who would betray Him as well. It was the lowest job imaginable for the leader of the universe, yet He not only did it willingly, He encouraged us to serve one another as well.

A godly leader will serve the body of Christ. He will look for opportunities to practice humility and to encourage the people he's leading to serve and love one another. It is easy to love and serve those who agree with our leadership; it is a whole other story to love and serve those who disagree with us. *That* is the sign of a good leader. If Jesus Christ could wash the feet of Judas Iscariot, can we not serve those who wish us harm and oppose our leadership for whatever reason?

As I mentioned, a godly leader will walk in humility. This can be done by practicing vulnerability, openness, and honesty! A leader who is honest about his faults can lead more effectively through weakness. Remember that His strength is made perfect in weakness (2 Corinthians 12:9).

These two things—servant leadership and humility—can help shape a godly leader. If we add to that our prayers for our leaders and those who are in authority over us, just imagine what kind of leaders we would see.

Taking It Deeper

1. The author mentions wanting "freedom" in church. What does that phrase mean to you?

2. Can you think of a time, or times when you experienced good and/or bad leadership?

3. Can you commit to setting aside time to pray for those in leadership over you? If not, what is holding you back?

4. What are some ways you can serve the leaders God has placed you under? If you are in a position of leadership, how can you wash the feet of those you are leading?

5. What does your ideal leader look like?

Father, I want to pray for those in leadership over me. Help me to see them as You see them. Allow me opportunities to "wash the feet" of those around me. As a leader, give me opportunities to serve others in humility and love. In Jesus' name, amen!

CHAPTER 6

Over There

I felt the call to missions from around the age of fifteen. When I was twenty-four, I went to Texas for a YWAM DTS. Founded in 1960 by Loren Cunningham, Youth With A Mission is an international, interdenominational Christian missionary organization. Its stated goal is to "know God and to make Him known." A Discipleship Training School generally lasts five to six months and consists of a three-month lecture/study phase followed by a two- to three-month evangelistic/service outreach, typically to a different culture, so that students can get a taste of missions and assist long-term missionaries in their work.

Our Discipleship Training School was large enough (forty-two students) that we were split into four groups. One went to the Native communities in the American Midwest, one to China, one to South Africa, and then there was my group. We went to Russia. We tried to psyche ourselves up to go to Russia in January/February. We knew it would be cold. We jokingly tried to build ourselves up by thinking how easy the others would have it while they were eating Chinese food, surfing, and hitting the shopping malls while we were the frozen chosen!

I had never been out of North America before and wasn't sure what to expect. We arrived in Moscow in January 1994. After a couple days and a twenty-four-hour train ride, we arrived in Perm, near the Ural Mountains, which was where we spent the next two months of outreach.

Pulling an All-Nighter

Overseas, it is common for church services to last a long time—some places, even overnight! There's a long service recorded in the New Testament as well:

"On the first day of the week, when we were gathered together to break bread, Paul talked with them, intending to depart on the next day, and he prolonged his speech until midnight. There were many lamps in the upper room where we were gathered. And a young man named Eutychus, sitting at the window, sank into a deep sleep as Paul talked still longer. And being overcome by sleep, he fell down from the third story and was taken up dead. But Paul went down and bent over him, and taking him in his arms, said, 'Do not be alarmed, for his life is in him.' And when Paul had gone up and had broken bread and eaten, he conversed with them a long while, until daybreak, and so departed. And they took the youth away alive, and were not a little comforted" (Acts 20:7–12).

We encountered some amazing church services in Russia, though I couldn't understand what was being said unless a translator was available. I remember one service in particular though. We had a team of missionaries from Latvia, our team, and the Russian people all gathered together singing the same worship song, each in his or her own language. The beauty of this moment was apparent and I found myself remembering the verse that talks about every tribe and tongue and nation (Revelation 7:9–10).

While in Russia, we encountered a faith that was real and I saw people who hungered for more of God! One service we went to started at 8:00 a.m. and included singing, prayers, and a sermon before repeating the cycle over and over with different speakers; even the young children were participating. At 1:00 p.m., people still lingered, though the service had been going for five hours!

Try doing that in a North American church service, where we have food in the oven before leaving for church and start looking at our watch if the preacher's still talking after twenty minutes! In fact, I was once asked to preach at a church in Canada and was told that no matter what time the worship ended, I needed to be done preaching by 11:55 so that the church worship team could play one last song before we dismissed promptly at noon!

No pressure!

In Russia, we were able to share in one town called Lysva, and the people of the church there took us into their homes individually, or in groups, as they were able. We stayed a few days and were made to feel very welcome. As we shared in the church, the people showered us with love. On the day we left, young adults ran beside the train throwing kisses and mimicking a play our group had done in which the characters had given their hearts away. In this instance, the people running by the train were miming that they were giving us their hearts! Little kids ran as long as they could as our train pulled away. Needless to say, even some of the men in our group shed some tears that day.

* * *

When we first arrived in Zagreb, Croatia, in 1996, I wasn't sure where we would attend church. We heard about a dual-language (English and Croatian) international service from local missionaries and decided to attend.

During our first period of time in Croatia, we spent many Sundays visiting this church. The pastor was a friendly Englishman who really cared about the people. As this was an international service, there were just as many foreigners as there were locals. However, the people seemed genuinely caring and many of the foreign military members, in the country as part of the UN peacekeeping forces, would attend as time allowed.

It was during our second journey to Croatia that we decided to stop attending this church. We had been visiting three churches on a regular basis, but when we returned from furlough, the pastor of this one asked if we would lead a cell group that met in the middle of the week. (In fact, he announced us as leaders before he even asked us.) The stipulation was that we would have to limit our involvement to the international church alone. We weren't prepared to make that commitment, as we felt the Lord still wanted us to be involved in some form with the other two Croatian churches we had been attending intermittently. At that point, we decided to go where our hearts were leading us and did not leave with hard feelings or resentment. Yet we were a bit sad that the international church couldn't see the body of Christ in a broader sense and support our involvement with other denominations.

* * *

KC was an interesting church. One of the leaders was very passionate about reaching the lost. His main interest lay in hosting evenings of poetry and song. He would heavily advertise these events and use either the church or a hall in town. People who attended were encouraged to come and visit the church at some point. The leader of this endeavor, Vlado, was a dear man of God who was an amazing writer in his own right. Over our time in Croatia, he invited us to share songs and poetry at these events.

We started off singing regularly, but my wife and I, not being professional musicians, didn't feel comfortable doing so. My wife is a great piano player, but we could not always find time to practice. The events were so close together and our schedules so busy that we often went with little to no preparation time. This would result in comical incidents where one or both of us would forget the words or lose our place in the middle of a set. Okay, it was only comical looking back, not at the time. I remember one time where we truly blew a whole song, butchering it and fumbling our way through. One of our coworkers had his face in his hands and we both wanted to crawl under the keyboard, but those in attendance still blessed us with their encouragement and applause.

Knowing that our music times were "challenging," I decided to focus on the poetry part of the events. I would write poems that my friend Vlado would translate into Croatian for me to read. I felt more comfortable sharing my own words and I learned some Croatian in the process.

One thing that seemed strange to me, and that I never got used to, was the mind-set about the use of music. People who were invited to the church for poetry evenings were encouraged to bring their instruments. Guitars, keyboards, and flutes were brought and used in the singing of songs during these evangelistic events. However, this particular church didn't believe in the use of instruments in their congregational worship times on Sunday mornings. All singing was a cappella.

I had never experienced worship without instruments and it was hard getting used to it. The folks at this church had a beautiful method of harmonizing, which we grew to love. We made dear friendships there that we still maintain to this day. We saw genuine love demonstrated, even by those who had been victims of the Balkan Wars. In fact, one refugee gave of her time to cook meals for the church staff and visitors. It seemed that whenever you came by to visit the church, Baka (Grandmother) Maria[2] was there to greet you with a kiss and a bowl of soup. Her friendly smile and heart of love warmed you as much as the soup did. We went back for a visit six years after we left and Baka Maria was still there, serving soup and giving of her time and love. She always had kind words to share and would dote over each visitor like they were her own grandchildren.

Other friends and staff members took time to visit, have a coffee, and discuss the Word of God. We probably met and worked with more people in this church than any other place we worked in Croatia. We were asked to participate in various church activities and outreach opportunities as they presented themselves. I would share from the pulpit occasionally, and we found ourselves helping in numerous areas.

---

2   This is the same Baka Maria introduced on Page 43

We would do everything from sorting Samaritan Purse shoeboxes for delivery to working in refugee camps and orphanages. I even dressed up as a clown with one of the other church workers, and once participated in a puppet show at an orphanage.

* * *

We became involved with KC due to the encouragement of another missionary. However, our involvement with EC was purely by "Godcidence." We were riding the bus to our neighborhood with a believer from KC when he looked over and recognized a fellow Christian who lived in our neighborhood and attended EC. Invites were given and my wife and I made our first trip on a Sunday evening to EC.

The church met in the basement of an apartment complex. The room wasn't large, but the service was quite packed. The pastor's daughter and two sons, in their teens at the time, would lead worship. These young adults were very friendly and passionate about God. They made us feel welcome, as did the entire congregation. We developed some very special friendships with the young adults in the church.

It was a bit harder to develop relationships with the elderly members. They must have heard about the saying, "Children should be seen and not heard," because they didn't seem too happy when babies were in the sanctuary. Oh, they seemed to enjoy the babies before the service would start. But once it began, if a baby made a noise, crawled on the floor, or even laughed, the bakas would give the parents stern looks and make noises that we knew, even without translation, meant, "Get your kids off the floor, and keep them quiet so we won't miss anything."

Once our daughter was born, we were on the receiving end of those looks and noises when she took off and began crawling up the aisle.

* * *

Once a month, all the Christian churches in Zagreb celebrated the Lord's Supper. These times partaking of Communion showed me the differences that can exist in the body of Christ, be they cultural or religious.

I grew up in a church culture that celebrated Communion, though not on a monthly basis. I thought I knew what to expect when I received the tiny cup of juice and little piece of bread.

Then I went to Croatia.

At the international service, they would do things the way I had been raised—what I refer to as the "normal" way. I felt comfortable in that setting and knew what to expect.

It was at the EC that my views of how Communion should happen received a radical shake-up. On the first Sunday evening where Communion was to take place, I looked for the little cups and the piece of bread. Instead, we were handed an actual loaf of freshly baked bread and encouraged to tear a piece off before passing it down the aisle and on back. My wife and I were in the last row, so we tore off a piece of what was left. Then I noticed something that made me a bit squirmy: they only had one cup. This large chalice came with a napkin. People would take a sip, wipe the lip of the cup, and hand it to the next person. My mind raced with possible health issues and reasons why this was too unsanitary. I admit to being a bit of a germaphobe, and by the time the cup reached us, there were *floaties* in it. At this point, I was hoping they'd used real wine so as to at least kill some of the germs. I wiped the cup lid fiercely and took the tiniest of sips, all the while hoping the fact that we could trample on snakes and scorpions meant we could also survive the bits of backwashed bread that had found their way into the wine as the congregation sipped.

The following month, my wife and I made a beeline to the first two seats in the front row. We knew it was Communion Sunday and we were prepared for a very sanitary experience with God!

Sure enough, the bread was passed and then the cup. My wife and I took the first sips and relaxed. Until, that is, the last person in the last row finished their sip and the cup was brought back to the front to start again so as not to waste any!

Ah, good times!

It seemed like no matter where we sat, we had floaties! One Sunday night, again sitting in the front, the cup was started in the back of the church! Do you think God was trying to tell us something? We sure did. We needed to repent of being self-seeking and truly, humbly, share with our brethren and sisters as they celebrated the sacrifice of Jesus. Looking back, we would love another chance to share communion with those followers of Christ who loved us despite our mistakes.

*   *   *

I was able to visit a church in the southern part of Croatia twice. The pastor had e-mailed us, begging YWAM to come visit. I took this as a Macedonian call and went willingly. The people were friendly, but the translator was the only one who spoke English. Their desire for God was huge and they were very gracious as I shared from the Word.

Later, when I returned with an outreach team, they again shared their hearts and home with us, supporting us as we shared the gospel in the streets.

*   *   *

Not every experience was a good one though. In the city where we worked the most, one of the local churches felt they had a duty to not only condemn and/or convert Catholics but to call them out while doing so. The pastor and members of his church would stand in the main square with a bullhorn and yell at the passersby who were leaving mass, telling them that they were going to hell!

This church would also produce and hand out literature stating the same message. One church asked me what I thought about the material. I likened it to a punch in the face. I said something along the lines of "If I punched you in the face, knocked you down, and then gave you my hand and said, 'Let me tell you about my friend Jesus,' would you listen to me?"

They had gotten many of their ideas from TV evangelists and we saw that come out in their prayers for healing. I once injured my back moving a washing machine downhill for a number of blocks on a small luggage dolly. (Hey, we had no car!) I asked this group for prayer, as we had been invited to a home service in our neighborhood. The pastor stretched my legs out and, with the people gathered around, declared that one of my legs was shorter than the other and that this was the cause of my pain. I tried to explain that my leg length was due to the way I was sitting, but it was to no avail. Repeatedly, the group laid hands on me, prayed, and then my legs would be rechecked. After this went on for some time, I realized if my leg did not stretch, I would be there all night. I am ashamed to admit it, but I finally adjusted the way I was sitting; my healing was proclaimed by the pastor and we left.

The next week, I was asked by one lady in the church if I had always walked with a limp due to the "shortness" of one leg. When I explained what had happened, she told the pastor, who declared that I lacked faith! Due to language barriers and a lack of confidence in my identity in Christ at the time, I didn't discuss my feelings with the pastor, and I regret that I may have missed an opportunity to help him see where he was in error. I also regret that I did not voice my concern during the actual prayer meeting.

As I mentioned previously, I was going through some personal issues which caused me to become hypercritical of the church at large. Even house churches were no longer the "right way" to me. I was nearing my death experience as my heart hardened to church as a whole.

I did have enough love in my heart though that I couldn't help but cry when, on our last Sunday in Croatia, the people at KC asked us to worship with them one last time. They surprised us as many stepped forward to share how they had been blessed and encouraged by our time there.

As we drove through our neighborhood, numerous neighbors, some we had never really known, came out onto the street and waved good-bye to us. Again, we had tears in our eyes.

Though the experiences were mostly good, I was headed into a dry and desolate place in my walk with the Lord. It was actually both the end and the beginning!

What I Learned on the Way to the Resurrection

6. The joy of the Lord truly is our strength!

Earlier, I mentioned the five-hour church services in Russia. Sitting through a five-hour service in a foreign language wasn't my idea of a fun Sunday. Hunger and thirst were two things I found to be a distraction. I passed the time by reading large portions of Scripture and trying to listen to the translators.

I often wondered what would motivate someone to sit and listen to a long—or in this case, *extremely* long—church service. I realize now that these people had the genuine joy of the Lord.

The Bible says that the joy of the Lord is our strength (Nehemiah 8:9–12). I believe there's a special joy from God that is given when people are in communion with Him.

Have you ever noticed how times of joy, happiness, and laughter seem to strengthen your overall body? I sure have. I've also noticed that when I'm worshipping the King of Kings and Lord of Lords, I feel stronger, more focused, and very content. Time passes without notice and everything else falls by the wayside when I'm in deep communion with the Lord.

Sarah once shared with me about a time when she communed with Christ at a ladies conference, after a time of ministry. As she fellowshipped with Jesus, listening to His heart for her, she felt nothing but His love and a desire to be with Him. She was then pulled out of her private worship time by a group leader telling her it was dinnertime. She was surprised to find everyone with their meals half-finished, yet she didn't feel hungry at all.

It's only when I get distracted by things around me, like how uncomfortable the seat is or how much time has passed, that I begin to grow weary and stressed. That weariness can lead to frustration, irritability, and even a critical spirit.

If the joy of the Lord is our strength, then the opposite is also true. Proverbs 17:22 (NIV) says, "A cheerful heart is good medicine, but a crushed spirit dries up the bones."

I remember watching people worship in one church in the United States. They would sing, "The joy of the Lord is my strength," with looks of sadness and misery on their faces. They rarely smiled, clapped half-heartedly, and seemed half-dead. I asked one pastor what he thought, as each week there would be no joy evident. This pastor said, "Halfway through a service, you (as the speaker) should start preaching a funeral service. If they notice, great, something positive might happen. If not, you should bury them and move on!"

How often are we half-dead in church? Or for that matter, half-asleep?

The joy of the Lord *is* our strength. Where do we find that joy? We find it at the feet of the Father! We should strive to focus on Him, to cling to Him, and to truly *worship* Him! Only then will we find true strength!

Taking It Deeper

1. At what point do you begin getting uncomfortable or distracted in church? Why?

2. The joy of the Lord is our strength. What does that statement mean to you?

3. Can you list three things in the church that give you joy?

4. Do you ever find yourself looking at your watch in church? Can you put it away next Sunday?

5. What are some other distractions you face in church? What can be done to minimize them?

Father, please help me to experience the strength that can only be found in You. Help me to experience joy in my heart as I worship You. Let my mind be focused without distraction on the things eternal and not on the things external. Allow me to linger in Your presence. In Jesus' name, amen.

CHAPTER 7

The End and the Beginning

I no longer had any interest in going to church. Having been burned, hurt, and finally, irritated by religion, I could no longer fake my displeasure at being involved with hypocrites! It just took a bit of time for it all to come to a head.

My return from the mission field hadn't gone as planned. I assumed many would want to hear about our time there and that we would be embraced by friends and family alike. The truth was, just as our life had moved on, so had everyone else's. Friends got married and moved away, had children, bought homes, began studies, and got new jobs. Our experiences in Croatia left us with reverse culture shock upon our

Debrief Them Please!

I think the body of Christ does a disservice to those who participate in ministry activity if they aren't properly debriefed.

When Paul and Barnabas returned to their sending church at the end of their first term of missionary service, they reported "all that God had done with them" (Acts 14:27).

It's important to allow those who have ministered a chance to share their stories. It's also important for someone to go deeper with them.

There is value in asking questions *and* listening to both the good and bad experiences those who minister the gospel have gone through.

return home and, unless you have experienced that, it's hard to relate to and understand.

I tried to get involved in church right away, and it was here that my wife and I led the church that closed and resulted in a children's church in our home. It was my last hurrah. When we moved, my wife wanted us to find a church, but my interest was dead.

My personal life, including sin I was hiding from the world, now overwhelmed me. I was truly tired of religious people and no one, no church, was above my indignation.

Of course, it didn't help that every attempt to find a church resulted in more and more frustration.

* * *

We walked in the door and were warmly greeted by the pastor. Members of the congregation also welcomed us and made us feel like it was appreciated that we were there.

The message was interesting, the size of the church was small (thirty or so people), and I found nothing to complain about that first Sunday visiting a new church.

The following week, as we entered the church, the pastor again greeted us, but he acted like it was the first time we had met. Okay, I could forgive that, as I am horrible with names myself. We reminded him that we had been there the week before and he seemed surprised. He then looked at our daughter and said something along the lines of "I thought she looked familiar."

The third Sunday, I was beginning to wonder if this would be a good fit for us. I wanted to give it a shot for my wife and daughter, as my wife had expressed a desire to attend regularly, but going to church felt like fingernails scraping across a chalkboard. As we walked in the door, the pastor again greeted us like he had never seen us before. This time I was a bit more irritated, as I thought three weeks was enough time in a small church for the pastor to at least realize we had been there more than once!

On the final Sunday of our attendance, we walked in the door and the pastor (you guessed it!) acted like we were first-time visitors and introduced himself to us yet again! To top it all off, on this particular Sunday, the pastor pointed out their church welcoming committee and congratulated them for how they always came to the homes of first-time visitors with a warm plate of cookies! My wife and I looked at each other and I couldn't help it ... I wanted to know where our cookies were. After four weeks, not only did the pastor still not recognize us, but apparently we were ghosts in the church, as no one had been by our house or called, though we had put our information down on the card given to us during our first visit there.

It sounds immature now, but for where I was at emotionally at that moment, the cookies were the last straw. As we left the church, I told my wife that four weeks without the pastor recognizing at least our faces, and the welcoming committee never welcoming us, was enough for me.

Being welcomed or greeted may seem like a minor deal, but it just didn't make us feel like we were actually wanted. I know others have experienced this type of thing as well. S. J. shared one such incident with me a little while ago.

> One church we tried was nice (as all churches are), but in the four Sundays we attended *not one person* talked to us—not even to say, "Hello, are you new?" or "I've never met you before." It wasn't a big church, maybe about 150 maximum each Sunday.
>
> —S. J.

*   *   *

I cannot explain how bad things were getting. I believe, looking back on it now, that I was suffering from depression. I also believe the reason had more to do with how I saw myself than anything else. I felt worthless, unloved, and burned out.

Things seemed to be falling apart. I was on an emotional downward spiral. We were broke and discouraged. In desperation, my wife pulled into a church parking lot. The church was huge. The building took up half a block and was so large you could literally drive under a walkway connecting parts of the building.

As Sarah pulled into the lot, I was sobbing with the weight of all that was on me at the time. She went up to the church where a few members were gathered outside and asked for someone to come and talk to me. One person said they weren't really qualified and asked if we were church members. She said no, that I just needed someone to talk to. They encouraged her to bring me back on a Sunday. My wife was nearly begging by this point, but again she was encouraged to bring me to the church on a Sunday when a pastor could talk with me.

*   *   *

One group of believers from another church—one I found difficult to enjoy for a variety of reasons—invited us to their house for a Bible study. We went. Though the people were friendly, I wasn't prepared to accept their love and friendship. In fact, I tried to paste on a smile for the benefit of my family, but I felt no real joy in going to these weekly gatherings. Though the people were nice, they kept asking us to attend various functions at their church.

At this point, I don't think I would have enjoyed *any* church service, no matter how nice everyone was and how "anointed" the pastor seemed to be.

I was at the end of my rope and felt like I was suffocating in the desert. It was at this point that I began to seriously talk about killing myself. My wife encouraged me to get help, but I refused to humble myself. I didn't really trust Christians at this point and felt that anything I shared could and would be used against me somehow. I also didn't want to show how weak and messed up I was. I mean, come on, I had been a missionary; how could I confess to being messed up?

After the umpteenth time of my threatening to kill myself, Sarah said that the next time I talked about suicide, she was going to call for help regardless of whether I wanted it or not.

Help was coming. On a day when the rain came down, my resurrection began.

*   *   *

Everything up until this point—every story and every thought—now came to a head. All of my experiences with "religion" had left me dry and parched. I hated church, hated Christians, and hated life.

When I gave my life to Christ on July 31, 1984, I asked Him to live in my heart as Savior. What I never acknowledged beyond lip service was that He was also Lord! I didn't give up control. My ticket was punched and I was going to heaven, and I believed that was all I really needed. I believed in God but acted like He didn't exist. I wasn't willing to give my life fully into His hands. That was all about to change.

As the rain came down, I stormed out of the house. I was tired, worn down, irritated, and angry. My struggle with unbelief and other sin was destroying my life, my wife and I were fighting continuously, and I wasn't happy at work, at home, or at church. I was ready for everything to be over.

I began driving down the road and contemplating which tree to ram my car into. Tears came down my face as I screamed at God! I was done. Life sucked!

Going around one corner, I finally screamed out a summary of what I felt! I sobbed uncontrollably, "I can't take it anymore!"

At that moment, the Lord broke through into my heart. I cannot explain it. There was nothing audible, yet I heard the Lord's voice clear as day. "This is what I've been waiting for. You are right. You can't take it, but I can."

It was like fireworks going off in my head. Suddenly, all those years of hearing about surrender, brokenness, and identity in Christ started to make sense.

I had an "Aha" moment.

The Lord then brought me into contact with a Christian brother who shared some deep biblical truths with me. What were these truths?

The first thing I learned was that God is a Father who cares.

> He will tend his flock like a shepherd; he will gather
> the lambs in his arms; he will carry them in his
> bosom, and gently lead those that are with young.
> —Isaiah 40:11

Our concept of God as a Father is shaped most often by our experiences, or lack thereof, with our earthly father. It may be hard to believe, but God is a Father to the fatherless and a defender of the widows! (Psalm 68:5).

God has our best interest at heart. Until we believe that, we're like cars without brakes. If we think God is only out to punish us and make our lives miserable, we're not seeing God for who He truly is.

You see, that's part of what I was doing. From my earliest experience, I was worried that I had disappointed God, that I could lose my salvation. This fear helped shape a view that God truly didn't care or have my best interest at heart.

You may be wondering why, if God had my best interest at heart, I went through these negative church experiences. It's a good question, and one I asked myself. It's also woefully misguided. It starts with the assumption that God either saw the experiences I went through and didn't care or that He was unable to stop them.

Both are wrong. God did see, He did care, and He could have stopped them. So why didn't He?

He had a better way. He redeemed the situation! You may have noticed that I've ended each chapter with things I learned on the way to the resurrection. There's a reason for that. Look at the stories found in the Bible: God could have given up on King David when he committed the sin of adultery. Instead, He redeemed that situation and the earthly heritage of Jesus Christ came through the line of David! In the New Testament, we see Peter messing up quite regularly and even denying the Lord on His way to the cross. Jesus didn't toss him aside and say that the experiences he went through disqualified him for further use. Instead, He redeemed the situation and Peter became "the Rock"!

Paul is another great example. Look at what he went through *after* he had an encounter with the living King of Kings.

> Are they servants of Christ? I am a better one—I am talking like a madman—with far greater labors, far more imprisonments, with countless beatings, and often near death. Five times I received at the hands of the Jews the forty lashes less one. Three times I was beaten with rods. Once I was stoned. Three times I was shipwrecked; a night and a day I was adrift at sea; on frequent journeys, in danger from rivers, danger from robbers, danger from my own people, danger from Gentiles, danger in the city, danger in the wilderness, danger at sea, danger from false brothers; in toil and hardship, through many a sleepless night, in hunger and thirst, often without food, in cold and exposure. And, apart from other things, there is the daily pressure on me of my anxiety for all the churches.
>
> —2 Corinthians 11:23–28

It would have been easy for Paul to blame God and say He was a Father who didn't care. Did He do that? Absolutely not! He saw how God redeemed the situation and used it for His glory. The same thing has happened with my past experiences. God has redeemed them and allowed me to share these stories and this truth with others ... including you!

Another thing I discovered was a secret—a secret so powerful that it changed my life. It started with John 3:16 (NIV).

> For God so loved the world that he gave his one and only Son, that whoever believes in him shall not perish but have eternal life.

Christ died for me and He took *all* my junk—all my fears, my doubts and insecurities, and my worries about the future. He took all of it to the cross. He banished death and gave us the hope of an eternal future with Him.

> Since the children have flesh and blood, he too shared in their humanity so that by his death he might destroy him who holds the power of death—that is, the devil—and free those who all their lives were held in slavery by their fear of death.
> —Hebrews 2:14–15 (NIV)

That answer led me to Galatians 2:20 (NIV).

> I have been crucified with Christ and I no longer live, but Christ lives in me. The life I live in the body, I live by faith in the Son of God, who loved me and gave himself for me.

This means that I died to sin. Christ took my sins, my life, to the cross. He is living in me now. He has been since I first gave my heart to Him.

Then I was shown Ezekiel 36:26 (NIV), which says,

> I will give you a new heart and put a new spirit in
> you; I will remove from you your heart of stone and
> give you a heart of flesh.

I found out that He had given me a new heart. Brand new! I became very excited by these truths, and as they began to soak into my heart, my life changed forever.

I discovered that all the things I struggled with, all the lies I believed, were just that—lies. God loved me, gave His life for me, and changed me. I still have problems that pop up in life. However, He has given me the strength to handle them. Suicide is no longer an option. A greater power and truth now operate in my life: God the Father, Jesus His Son, and the great comforter, the Holy Spirit. I was a *new* creation in Christ Jesus. No longer was I under the law. I had freedom!

How does that freedom apply to the church? Keep reading! Until we get there, remember that God has redeemed the experiences. This chapter does not end with a lesson I learned on the way to the resurrection. Jesus broke through my stubbornness and I began to truly experience the resurrection!

Taking It Deeper

1. Have you ever felt like giving up completely?

2. What does Jesus as "Lord" mean to you?

3. Read and reflect on Galatians 2:20. How can you apply that verse to your life?

4. Are you willing to let Jesus heal the pain of your past and to make all things new?

5. Who do you need to forgive as you move forward in your healing journey?

Father, I need a resurrection. I have been living in pain for far too long. I want You to bring me to a place where You are my everything. All that I am, all that I have, I lay at Your feet. I surrender my life completely into Your hands. In Jesus' name, amen.

CHAPTER 8

Refreshing

We decided to try a new church. An old high school friend had invited us to her church and we had just recently met a man from the church prayer team as well.

It was with a bit of nervousness that we entered PCOG. We were greeted by numerous people that Sunday morning. We found a place in the sanctuary, about halfway back, and I began looking over their church bulletin. As far as bulletins go, this one was fairly standard: men's prayer breakfast, Wednesday Bible study, youth groups ... It was all there. I love church bulletins. You really can get a feel for what a church is all about by the activities and notices in the bulletin. Is prayer a focus? Do they have a youth group? Are they reaching out across all economic, cultural, and gender lines? PCOG seemed to be focusing on many of these areas.

The worship leader began leading the praise team that Sunday and my wife and I really enjoyed the familiar songs. Around the time that many churches would be wrapping up the praise and worship, I began to look for the pastor to come up and begin the message. He never came. Instead, on this Sunday, we sang and sang and, yes, sang some more. Finally, after the worship had lasted as long as most church services, the pastor stood up and said that the Lord was doing something, so we should just enjoy the worship. He sat back down and we sang some more worship songs before church was finally dismissed. The fact that the pastor stood up, gave a Scripture, and then encouraged people to keep singing was very inspiring to me. He willingly laid aside his message for worship! That spoke more to me than any sermon would have at that point.

We left that day and I turned to my wife, saying, "Okay, we have to come back. I enjoyed the worship and would love to hear the pastor share a message." The entire drive home we talked about that service, and we both felt such a peace and joy.

We came back the next week. In fact, I was itching to go. Whereas before my crisis point, I was no longer truly interested in church attendance, I was now on the opposite side of the spectrum. I wanted to be there. The pastor shared a message that impacted us and again made way for what the Spirit was doing, this time by allowing some members of the congregation to share things the Holy Spirit was impressing upon them. His humility, vulnerability, and direct way of speaking were quite inspirational. We decided then and there to give this church a longer chance. As God was changing me, I also changed in how I approached my view of church. I was truly listening for the first time in a long, long time. I was able to put aside my checklist of prejudgments and no longer felt that open disdain that I was feeling before the encounter with the Lord that I detailed in the last chapter. Instead, I was able to hear the message and worship the Lord without hindrance or distraction.

We came back again and again, and God slowly chipped away the wall I had placed around my heart. My daughter really enjoyed the children's church, and the pastor of that ministry always made her feel welcome. He made sure that she felt included in the children's church. In fact, everyone seemed genuinely friendly and caring. We were always greeted warmly and people took time to talk with us. We were made to feel included, and it did not feel as if anyone was judging or ignoring us. When services were over, there wasn't a huge bolt for the door. People lingered, talked, and made plans to get together throughout the week. The love I saw emanating from this group seemed genuine and infectious.

I think if people would spend more time in (and out) of our churches genuinely showing how much they care for each other and visitors alike, we could make a powerful impact. It had a significant impact in our lives and we're not the only ones.

You may remember S. J., who shared an earlier experience of being ignored at one church her family attended. She said that just the opposite occurred in the next church her family visited. I'll let her tell the story.

> Even in the first few Sundays, various people during "community time" came and chatted with us, showing genuine interest in who we were, where we lived, etc. Community was done after worship and before announcements, where you go and get coffee or tea and meet people. This wasn't just an obligatory, awkward, "Turn around and shake hands with the people around you" sort of thing. People were genuine, real, and truly interested. It was so refreshing and made us feel so welcome.
>
> —S. J.

I read what S. J. shared and I am reminded of how Jesus was always able to make people feel welcomed, cared for, and loved. He showed concern for both the multitudes and the individual. We can learn something from that. Reaching out in genuine love and interest can change a life.

Honour One Another

"Love one another with brotherly affection. Outdo one another in showing honour" (Romans 12:10).

It takes a bit of work, but when we try to learn something about the people God brings us into contact with, we show them honor.

We also honour others when we show them respect and consider them and their needs before our own.

I remember at work a few years back, I was manning the register during an employees lunch break. An older gentleman came in and looked sad. I asked him how he was doing and he responded that I probably didn't care but was just asking that as many people seem to do. When I assured him I was genuinely interested and had noticed that he looked down, he shared that he was about to have surgery and was nervous about the upcoming procedure. I asked if I could pray with him and he seemed pleasantly surprised by my offer. So right there in the thrift store, I prayed for his health, his concerns, and that the Lord would guide the surgeon's hands. He thanked me and left. Months later, he returned to tell me that he went into the surgery with no fear and thanked me again for praying with him. I got to know this gentleman quite a bit over the next few years and enjoyed the numerous conversations we had. I would have missed those times if I had not reached out in genuine interest.

Who might God be calling you to reach out to?

*   *   *

Let's return to the story of this new church the Lord had brought us to.

The day finally came when I looked at my wife as we left the church and said something I *never* thought I would say. I asked, "When are we going to join this church?" I don't know which one of us was more surprised by my question!

We talked about the implications of joining a church and what it would mean to us. After years of being hurt by the people in the churches I attended, I wanted to make sure I was committed to the idea. I wanted to be involved and not just a member in name only.

We approached the pastor about membership and were given a list of the church's beliefs. In the past, I would have taken this list, read it, and then run in the opposite direction. Instead, my wife and I went through the list of twenty items the church stood on. We did not do a quick read but truly discussed where we stood on each statement of faith. In addition to helping find clarity on whether this was the church for us, by going through each of the twenty items and discussing them, it allowed my wife and me to connect in conversation. We found that we were in complete agreement with eighteen of the items on the list and felt the other two weren't major enough for us to make an issue about them.

We told the pastor we were committed to taking the plunge, and on "New Member" Sunday, my family was welcomed into the fold of PCOG. We were impressed when, after the service, all the new members were invited to a lunch at the church. The pastor's wife not only had learned everyone's names but knew something about every new member. The fact that she had made a point of learning about an interest, hobby, or job really spoke volumes to us. The pastor's wife made everyone feel special. It reinforced the feeling of acceptance and care we had noticed over and over again at PCOG.

We never know how a word, greeting, or acknowledgment can impact people in a positive *or* negative manner for all eternity. Consider this story I was sent recently:

> As a college student, I tried to get involved with a local church. I joined as a member, taught fifth grade Sunday school, and led the junior high music time. It was a rather large church. As far as Sunday school went, no parents ever introduced themselves and the children behaved very badly (fistfights, jumping out of the window, etc.). The music time didn't go that well, but at least everyone behaved.
>
> I thought I was really trying to plug into the church, but it seemed as though no adults even noticed or appreciated me. I left for two months to student-teach in another state, and when I came back to church afterward, my mailbox was gone. I was hurt! No one had thanked me for all the work I had put in or tried to contact me before taking

away my mailbox. I felt invisible! Thankfully, I've
had many more good experiences than poor ones,
but that one stuck out to a college student who was
really making an effort.

—A. M.

Thankfully, the experience A. M. had didn't turn her against the
Lord. How often do we think about how others might be impacted
by our words or lack thereof? How would our conversations change
if we remembered that they could have impact for eternity? Would
we regret not greeting the ones we often ignore?

At PCOG, the people seemed to go out of their way in getting
to know us. It made us feel comfortable and paved the way for what
happened next.

*   *   *

I have mentioned more than once a struggle with a certain sin
that was greatly affecting my life. Our new pastor shocked me one
day when he addressed that particular sin directly from the pulpit.
That day, God began a work that was to bear fruit in my life before
too long.

I went into my first men's breakfast with some trepidation. Not
sure what to expect, but having been warmly invited by more than
one man, I slipped in the door and made for the table in the far
back. When everyone had gathered, the food was blessed and we all
went for heaping plates of breakfast foods. I was beginning to relax
and enjoy myself.

That's when a gentleman, whom I will refer to as Clark, stood
up to share a few words about his life as we finished our breakfast.
Clark shared his struggle with the habitual sin of pornography. I was
shocked that someone would share such revealing details in a church
setting. Sure, the pastor talked about it, but hearing someone talk
more personally about it spoke volumes to me.

Having been conditioned to not trust people in church with the "deep" things in life, I was waiting for the response his confession would create. What I saw were men reaching out with love and compassion. Many shared their own struggles and they prayed for one another.

I left that morning unable to get the thought of what I had seen out of my head. I repented of my own sin, and it wasn't very long before I began to confess the sin to my wife—and to Clark as well. God used that situation to begin a work of healing in my life. Over the years since this day, I have been able to speak in churches about my own struggle with pornography and to counsel many men who were struggling with this issue. My struggle did not go away overnight, but as I said, the healing started that day over breakfast.

Whereas I once shunned the whole thought of participation, I now found an increased desire to be in church. The men's breakfast became a place of spiritual refreshing. My wife and I began to participate in more of the activities the church had to offer. We didn't miss an opportunity to join others.

My wife joined the choir. She has always been a worshipper at heart. Over the years, she has written numerous worship songs that speak of her desire for more of the presence of God. I enjoyed watching her sing on a Sunday morning and would come to the practices every time I could. For myself, I started off helping with the PowerPoint projector but got so caught up singing the worship songs that I would often forgot to change the slides from one song to the next. Before long, I was standing with my wife in the choir. In fact, the choir director said he had been wondering when I would make the switch.

Sarah had been praying for me for a long time. One day, before my resurrection, while she was visiting another church with friends, they had a special prayer time with a guest speaker. He asked her what she wanted prayer for and she responded that her prayer was that one day God would do the work needed in our lives so that we could be in fruitful ministry together. Now, months later, we were both part of the worship team, and she was excited to see how God had answered her prayer. It felt like we were connecting on a new level and falling in love with each other all over again.

We were involved up to our ears in PCOG and loving every minute of it. If things popped up that bothered me, whereas in the past I would have walked away, I was able, with the Lord's help, to look past them and see God in the midst. As you can see from the lessons learned on the way to the resurrection that I ended earlier chapters with, the Lord was able to heal my past as well.

So imagine how saddened we were the day God called us to leave.

* * *

We had felt God "stirring our nest" for some time and knew He was calling us to move on. At the time, there were many options on the table. We looked at going back to Croatia or moving to Oregon or Niagara Falls to be near aging grandparents. We prayed about staying in Tennessee and applying as house parents at a children's home affiliated with our church. Each time we prayed, the Lord seemed to close the door on one of the options.

The one thing that kept coming up in our prayer time was the one item we hadn't actually been praying about—moving to northern British Columbia, Canada. We prayed repeatedly about this once we felt the Lord might be moving us in that direction. We met with our pastor and talked with him about the decision, asking for his prayers and counsel. Finally, it became clear that the Lord most definitely wanted us to go to British Columbia, and not just BC but specifically my wife's hometown of Smithers.

My wife and daughter went to Smithers a few months before I did. I had to finish up my job, start counseling training, and put what stuff we did not give away into storage for a time. After my job ended, I packed the van and made my way north to join my family.

* * *

We had visited KBF a few times over the years when on furlough from the mission field. When our daughter was born, one family from this church showed up at our house with a birthday cake and balloons. A group of women also hosted a baby shower for her. We found those little touches by individual members to be very endearing. We also enjoyed frequent barbeques and fun gatherings.

I think, for me, I enjoyed the style of service at KBF more than anything else. KBF was located in a First Nations community and was really a missionary church. That appealed to me a lot. The pastor always spoke from his heart and was vulnerable with everyone in the fellowship. He and his wife had a very good standing in the community and people genuinely cared about them.

Interaction and community involvement at all levels can impact how people see a church. That's what happened with one friend.

> I had met the new pastor at my old church over the summer, while staying in my hometown. I was playing slow-pitch softball for my former team and the new pastor was playing on second base. He was very approachable and down to earth and I enjoyed him as a teammate. I had really grown to enjoy him out of the pulpit. I eventually moved thirty miles from this church but decided that the early Sunday morning trips were well worth it.
>
> He had great messages, his points were explained quite well, and I felt like I was being "taught" instead of being "preached at."
>
> —R. M.

At KBF, I liked the fact that services were what I would consider atypical. There was a start time, but we tended to start casually, a bit later, as was considered culturally acceptable. (That part was never easy for me, as I am very time-conscious.) People would grab their cup of coffee and find a seat. Typically, when I was there, the chairs were set in a round or U-shaped pattern. The pastor and a few others would grab their guitars and people would call out song numbers from the booklets handed out at the start of every service. There was no set time for the singing, and it was sometimes longer and sometimes shorter, but it was always enjoyable.

The messages at KBF tended to be like expository walks through books of the Bible. A book would be chosen and the pastor, or another member, would lead people through a verse-by-verse look at that book over several Sundays before moving to another book. I learned a lot during this time.

I liked that it was very participatory. People were encouraged to ask questions and discuss the message and Scriptures. In many ways, it felt like a Bible study, but it seemed much more engaging.

In many ways, KBF was a place of rest and refreshing. We didn't have lots of expectations placed on us and we were able to just relax and be ourselves. It was the perfect setup for the next phase and stage of our life.

Things I Learned *after* the Resurrection

1. God truly wants His children to rest.

I mentioned that KBF was a place of rest. PCOG was as well. In fact, it seemed that after God began restoring our marriage and teaching us about our identities in Him, He allowed us a long season of rest and restoration. The Bible talks about rest for God's children:

> So then, there remains a Sabbath rest for the people of God, for whoever has entered God's rest has also rested from his works as God did from his.
> —Hebrews 4:9–10

> For it is by grace you have been saved, through faith—and this not from yourselves, it is the gift of God—not by works, so that no one can boast. For we are God's workmanship, created in Christ Jesus to do good works, which God prepared in advance for us to do.
> —Ephesians 2:8–9 (NIV)

You may remember the story I shared in the beginning of this book about how, shortly after my salvation, the assistant pastor made a comment that I took to heart: I began to fear the loss of my salvation as doubt and worry crept in.

This experience led to my continually striving to "prove" myself to God. I figured that witnessing for Him would earn His pleasure. Later, as a missionary, I thought that maybe *now* I was doing enough. The feelings continued year after year. Though I didn't feel accepted myself, I still spent time in pastoral ministry and continually told others about Him! The reason I had no peace was that I kept trying to earn something I already had.

John 3:16 says that if we believe in Him, we will have eternal life. We are accepted! I no longer have to strive. In fact, by striving to earn a gift God already gave, I was making a mockery of His gift! All I have to do is receive it and rest! I didn't have to perform like a trained circus animal to earn His love, mercy, and forgiveness. I already have it.

I needed to enter that rest.

Instead of working to earn His pleasure, I needed to live in relationship with Him. When I worship Him, spending time growing in my relationship, I learn His heart and thoughts. Out of that, work flows naturally.

Taking It Deeper

1. Can you think of a time when someone spoke a word of encouragement at just the right moment? How did that impact you?

2. Who are the people you see regularly but do not truly know that you can speak words of encouragement to?

3. Read and reflect on Psalm 23. How can you apply that verse to your life?

4. What does rest mean to you?

5. Do you know that you are loved, accepted, and cared for by Jesus Christ?

Father, I need a refreshing in my life. Help me to know what it means to linger in Your presence, to drink from the living water and to rest under the shadow of Your wings. Help me to be encouraged and to be an encourager to those You bring me into contact with. In Jesus' name, amen.

CHAPTER 9

Recovery!

I survived the Blizzard of '93!

The storm struck in March and left Tennessee in a mess. I remember listening to the radio as the snow fell and hearing all the calls for rescue vehicles. Power lines fell, people were stranded, and the salt trucks couldn't keep up. All told, the storm did $6.6 billion in damages. In East Tennessee, we received a little over ten inches of snow. That summer, people wore "I Survived the Blizzard of '93" T-shirts.

In Canada, where I now live, ten inches doesn't qualify as a blizzard. In fact, when I share the Tennessee story here, people in BC even chuckle a little. Okay, they actually chuckle a lot. When snow or cold snaps happen in the Deep South, I will see friends on Facebook talking about how bad it is. Usually, it is twenty to twenty-five degrees Fahrenheit colder here than there. The snow is also a lot less comparatively. However, it's all about perspective. Tennessee doesn't get much snow. They have very few salt trucks. Some winters there, you can wear T-shirts in December. Ten inches of snow is very bad for an area not used to snow. It is hard for people not used to driving in that weather to suddenly have to deal with snow and ice.

Perspective.

My perspective on church began changing after I started walking out my identity in Christ. I no longer looked back on the past with pain and anger. I no longer thought of the people I encountered as hypocrites, nor did I feel the need to sit in judgment over their actions. This is not to say that every encounter was excusable, but I understand now that we truly live in a fallen world. The problem was not the church, or for that matter the people in the church. The problem was that I was looking at things from the wrong perspective.

I responded to many situations out of my own hurt and bitterness. The bitterness crept into my heart and colored my perspective and my actions. I was not looking at these situations with the eyes of Christ. Every story is redeemable. The worst person on earth still has the chance for redemption through Jesus Christ. There is nothing God cannot heal and use for His glory. As we near the end of this story I have been sharing, you will hopefully see the redemption Jesus Christ worked in my own life.

*   *   *

After spending a season at KBF, we watched the church community in Smithers, and across the north, come together in support of Rising Above. Rising Above is a Christian-based, registered charitable organization offering hope and healing from a biblical perspective to First Nations people across Canada. It is a First Nations ministry reaching out to First Nations people.

Rising Above focuses heavily on helping those hurt by residential school abuse, sexual abuse, and who struggle with addictions. The impact of this ministry has seen lives changed and many seeing not only a healing of past wounds but also finding a deeper relationship with Jesus Christ.

I had the honor of sitting on the planning committee that helped to organize the event in Moricetown, BC, and was blessed to see the lives touched and the intense follow-up with those who attended. The Lord used this time to show me how the body of Christ can work together to impact the nations for Him! Churches worked together without their own agendas, desiring to see lives changed.

It was not the first time I had seen that here in the Smithers area. A little over five years prior to this event, the churches in the Smithers region also worked together to facilitate a Billy Graham Evangelistic Association event in the local arena. Many came to Christ through this event. I fully believe the unity that the body of Christ displayed, with the addition of copious amounts of prayer, is still having an impact today.

Shortly after the Rising Above event, I was invited to preach at SBC. I took a couple of services while the pastor was on vacation. Upon his return, he announced he was moving south to pastor another church. I began helping out at SBC and was one of the men called on to take services during their pastoral search. Though I thought I was prepared at the time, I was not yet ready for full-time pastoral ministry.

We began spending more time at SBC and knew that would mean we had to pull back from KBF. We enjoyed our season at KBF but knew it was the right time to leave. I have fond memories of our time there and believe that the Lord used the people at KBF to continue the healing He was doing in my life. What happened next was to have a profound impact on my life.

*   *   *

When we moved to Canada, I was not able to work for the first couple of years. My wife being Canadian and my daughter being born here, it made sense for me to apply to become a landed immigrant. Though I am proud of my cultural background, I knew the Lord was calling us here longer than I could stay on a visitor visa. I helped homeschool my daughter, furthered my counseling training, and volunteered where I could. The day came when my paperwork was nearing final approval. I had asked the local ministerial, of which I was a part, to pray for me as I would be looking for a part-time job once the paperwork was finally approved. A few days later, after everything went through, I was on my way to the stationery store to make copies of my résumé when I ran into the local director of the Salvation Army.

He asked how things went, and after a brief conversation, I told him I was on my way to get my resume printed. He immediately offered me a job in the food bank. I was stunned but praised the Lord for His provision. I began working at the food bank and, after the building was renovated a few months later, helped create a drop-in center as well.

One ministry I also became involved in was a Saturday night street church at the Salvation Army. With soup, songs, and the Word, the street church was reaching out to the homeless and disenfranchised population.

Once SBC hired a pastor, my family began attending the Saturday night street church at the Salvation Army. I was one of four men who rotated sharing messages after the soup was served and people's bellies were full.

Though it was not without its challenges, we enjoyed participating in the street church community.

There came a point, however, when the leadership team felt it was time to cease this particular ministry. The number of people coming to the service had dwindled to the point where we had more volunteers than attendees.

* * *

After much prayer and waiting on God, my wife and I felt God calling us to step out in faith and proceed with plans He had been laying on our hearts. I approached my boss at the Salvation Army to see if we could use the facility. With permission given, we launched an endeavor I would never have thought about stepping into, considering my past experiences.

We were going to plant a church!

A lot of things went through my mind when the Lord called us in this ministry direction. The first was *Why me?*

Our town already had a lot of churches and I wasn't convinced we needed another one. I had been working with the other ministers on a regular basis and also wanted to assuage any thoughts that we might be "stealing sheep."

My wife and I laid down a vision of who we wanted to minister to and what kind of church we were looking at. I met with the ministerial and talked about our plans to launch this new church. We believed God was calling us to make a place for those with barriers that might keep them from participating in one of the other congregations in our community.

I was still working part time with the Salvation Army, but my wife and I were also working part time with Youth With A Mission again. The idea for the church, after consulting with my boss at the Salvation Army, was that we would partner in this endeavor. The Salvation Army, represented by my boss, would provide the space and the materials, as well as share in leadership, and I (as a YWAM missionary) would take primary lead in sharing the Word, while my wife led worship.

We wanted to reach out to those who didn't feel comfortable in a traditional church setting. Specifically, this meant reaching out to those who had been "burned" by church in one way or another. We also wanted a place where these people could come and be a part of a fellowship of believers. We hoped that it would be a welcoming place for people of all nations, for families, for singles, for the young and the old. We wanted to send a message that said, "We want you here. You matter to us and to God."

Thus was born Main Street Christian Fellowship.

I thought I knew where this journey would take us, but I was wrong. God used this experience to further cement the resurrection He began in my life all those years ago on a rain-slicked country road.

We tried to make our services a mix of the many things I had learned on the way to the resurrection. All those lessons at the end of each chapter of this book were included somehow in our teaching. I wanted to make the services interactive and engaging. For example, I would share what I liked to call "scratch-and-sniff" sermons, an idea borrowed from a *Discipleship Journal*. Basically, I read a text and then, using a whiteboard, talked about scratching below the surface and sniffing out clues from the story. Using the five senses, what would the person in the text have seen, tasted, heard, smelled, and touched? This allowed for feedback and interaction during the message with the people in attendance. I would then use what they shared and lead them to the point of my message. This worked well in small settings. I am not sure that level of connection and interaction would work in a larger church setting.

> **Numbers Game**
>
> One thing my wife and I don't care about is how many people come to the church every week.
>
> Our weekly prayer is that we want Him to bring out only those who need to hear that week's message.
>
> We want to follow Christ's example of impacting individual lives—the woman at the well, the one caught in sin, those needing healing. He changed individual lives. We are just as happy to share with one as we are fifty-one!

From delivering these scratch-and-sniff sermons to changing up the order of service, to congregational participation in the message, we tried to keep things open so that newcomers felt welcomed and the regulars enjoyed their time of worship, prayer, and the Word. I've heard from many over the years who enjoyed being involved in these services.

S. J. shares just one more story on that theme when discussing what keeps her family interested in their church:

> The church has clear, honest, and genuinely, openly presented sermons each week. They also have a different worship team each week—encouraging

those with musical talent to be part of the pool of musicians. It's often a group of young people leading worship. There's never a sense of a "worship pastor" always directing how things go, though one of the pastors does oversee the worship. In fact, one of the values of the church is to recognize and release gifts in the congregation, which is another thing that really appeals to me. There's no sense of the pastors knowing everything and being and doing everything; we are all one body with various gifts.

—S. J.

So we tried to incorporate our services in a way that allowed for participation. Yet we still made mistakes. We are human. Though I strived to keep from making the same kinds of mistakes I have shared in this story, I know we as a church—and I as a pastor—have made and will continue to make mistakes. My wife and I hope that even when we do make mistakes, God will redeem the situation, just as He has done for us.

My goal in life is to go deeper with Christ. I have made peace with my past and forgiven those in the church who hurt me. Though I was nearly killed by the church, I was resurrected spiritually by Christ.

Today, I am a man on a mission. I want to be a *real* witness of Christ, warts and all. I want people to see that Christians are human. We make mistakes; we hurt others and have been hurt ourselves. We aren't perfect, but we shouldn't use that as an excuse. We should be imitators of Christ.

If we can do that, our churches and our lives will never be the same.

I would love to say this is where the story ends, but God is not finished writing it yet. My journey continues. In the last chapter, I want to share a significant event that has forever altered my life and left me with no doubt that I am a new creation in Christ Jesus.

Things I Learned *after* the Resurrection

2. We should keep our eyes on Jesus, the author and finisher of our faith.

Why do we love the law so much? As a new Christian, you may recall that I was given a list of rules to follow. I have noticed over and over throughout my Christian walk that many Christians seem to enjoy being in bondage! We must, for why else would we try to live under the *law* when God sent His Son so we can have freedom?

This laundry list of law is even made into cute children's songs. "Be careful, little eyes, what you see!" It also talks about being careful what you do and say, where you go, and even what you think! I wonder why we're teaching our kids to live a life of Christian bondage. Not that we shouldn't guard our hearts and our flesh from sin, but perhaps we would naturally do that if our focus was on the greatness and mercy of Jesus!

Christ was born under the law, and His death made the way for our freedom!

Jesus showed how hard it was to follow the law when He mentioned things like anger, lust, and other commandments. That whole "Pluck your eyeballs out" and "Chop your hand off" thing really shows the futility of following the law. The law is good for one thing: to point out our need for a Savior. We see and become aware of sin even more when we look to the law. Try to live by the law and you'll find you are living a life filled with *no joy!*

Let me explain what I mean by the law. I've met Christians who literally try to keep the Old Testament laws. They follow the Old Testament dietary restrictions, Sabbath rules, etc. to the point that they become legalistic in their interpretation. Ultimately, they are putting themselves under the law!

> These rules may seem wise because they require strong devotion, pious self-denial, and severe bodily discipline. But they provide no help in conquering a person's evil desires.
>
> —Colossians 2:23 (NLT)

We cannot expect adherence to the law to make us holy and clean. When we try to bind ourselves to something Christ set us free from, are we not in effect saying that His death and resurrection aren't enough to make us clean?

After we receive Christ, we're no longer under the law (Romans 6:14). We're free from the law (Romans 6:7). We are *dead* to the law (Romans 7:4). In fact, my favorite verses in Romans are found in 8:1–2, which say,

> There is therefore now no condemnation for those who are in Christ Jesus. For the law of the Spirit of life has set you free in Christ Jesus from the law of sin and death.

Look at these Scriptures in Galatians:

> For all who rely on works of the law are under a curse; for it is written, "Cursed be everyone who does not abide by all things written in the Book of the Law, and do them." Now it is evident that no one is justified before God by the law, for "The righteous shall live by faith." But the law is not of faith, rather "The one who does them shall live by them." Christ redeemed us from the curse of the law by becoming a curse for us—for it is written, "Cursed is everyone who is hanged on a tree."
>
> —Galatians 3:10–13

Now before faith came, we were held captive under the law, imprisoned until the coming faith would be revealed. So then, the law was our guardian until Christ came, in order that we might be justified by faith. But now that faith has come, we are no longer under a guardian, for in Christ Jesus you are all sons of God, through faith.

—Galatians 3:23–26

For if you are trying to make yourselves right with God by keeping the law, you have been cut off from Christ! You have fallen away from God's grace.

—Galatians 5:4 (NLT)

This does not give us a license to sin! Paul addresses that in Romans.

What then? Are we to sin because we are not under law but under grace? By no means!

—Romans 6:15

Freedom in Christ does not mean we should practice stupidity.

Someone may say, "I'm allowed to do anything," but not everything is helpful. I'm allowed to do anything, but not everything encourages growth.

—1 Corinthians 10:23 (GW)

In order to grow in our relationships with God, we need to seek first the kingdom of God (Matthew 6:33) and know nothing but Jesus Christ and Him crucified (1 Corinthians 2:2). We'll find that as we focus on Him in worship and prayer, His heart becomes our heart. We'll also find that as we seek Him, He renews our mind. I'm not thinking about sin when I'm focused on Christ!

As I said at the beginning of this chapter, we should keep our eyes on Jesus, the author and finisher of our faith!

Taking It Deeper

1. What aspects of your church (or if you are not in a church right now, church in general) do you enjoy the most?

2. Are you open to God using you within the body of Christ as He sees fit?

3. How would you define law vs. grace?

4. Which of those do you feel you have experienced more of?

5. Spend time meditating on 1 Corinthians 2:2. What does it mean to you to know nothing but Jesus Christ and Him crucified?

Father, as we near the end of our journey together in this book, I ask that You would help me to remember that You purchased me with a price, that I am not my own, and that You have a plan for my life laid out before the foundations of this world. Help me to know Your grace and mercy in a real way and to display that same grace and mercy to others. In Jesus' name, amen.

CHAPTER 10

New Beginnings

I was happy where Main Street Christian Fellowship was going but, truth be told, was still a bit rebellious. I now spoke often on identity in Christ and felt that the Lord had healed so much of my past. I would share many of the lessons that I spoke about in this book and tried in my own strength to make our church as "unchurchlike" as possible.

I was proud that our services were not "traditional" and even enjoyed being a bit of a rebel. I loved to overturn the apple cart of expectation that people might have had about what a traditional church services looked like. I took the "resurrection" I had been given and ran in the opposite direction.

Pride had replaced pain.

I still had another lesson to learn.

Main Street Christian Fellowship was growing, faster than I had anticipated. After starting off slowly, we began seeing more and more people attend services. Those numbers became to me a sort of validation that we were on the right track. Where I used to not care about numbers, I started to become consumed by them. I am ashamed to say that I was missing out on the individual lives the Lord was bringing into our path.

Change started off slowly but a series of events began to transpire that picked up steam and caused my life to crash through the walls I had carefully constructed around my heart.

*   *   *

Pregnant!

This was the news my wife delivered to me one evening as I was winding down for the day. We were expecting a new baby. I was happy and confused, ecstatic and terrified. Our daughter was eleven and suddenly we were going to have a new child in our lives. I was twenty-seven when my daughter was born. I would be thirty-nine when my son was born. I wasn't old, but I was no longer a spring chicken.

I had been working part time for the Salvation Army still and with Youth With A Mission. I knew that this change in our life would mean my wife would have to stop working for a season and I would need to earn more than I was as a part-time missionary and food bank employee.

With all this in mind, I felt I should turn in my notice at the food bank and find full-time work. That very day my boss informed me he was going to be transferring to another town. I held off on my decision as we discussed the implications for this ministry unit. Within a couple of days, the area commander for the Salvation Army asked me if I would be willing to step into the role of director for the Bulkley Valley unit. I would be responsible for two thrift stores and food bank locations as well as the other ministry and social work happening in our unit. I prayed about it and felt that I should say yes.

Within a few short weeks, I was now leading our ministry unit and feeling way over my head. I was still trying to work PT with YWAM and that decision made things even more challenging. I was not getting paid with YWAM so there was no financial conflict of interest, but my heart was divided.

During this time, the church began to peak in attendance and I was torn as to what was YWAM work and what was Salvation Army.

As I struggled with my twin roles, I was not fully committed to either. I loved YWAM and felt it was a good fit but also loved my job, though I was not convinced I was cut out for it long term. My rebelliousness and scars from the past sill lingered and I began to examine both YWAM and the Salvation Army in light of my experiences. Though I believe God fully healed my past, I fell back on old patterns and started looking at these "religious" organizations in different ways.

It was during this time I also began working on the ideas for this book. I spoke, preached, and discussed these ideas with others, including my area commander at the time. Then one day, I sat down and poured out this story. In three months, I had the spine of his book completed. I naively thought it was 100 percent complete. I had the book edited and even entered it in a writing contest. I picked up endorsements but could not find a publisher. I now see the book wasn't finished. The ending wasn't right.

Then I got hit in the head.

Literally.

My third diagnosed concussion left me rattled.

For the first few months after this concussion, I found myself fatigued, confused, emotional, and struggling to make it through each day. My symptoms lingered as I went back to work and tried to do my job as well as pastor the church each week.

Our church attendance had been declining for some time, and just as I took pride in its growth, I was discouraged by the number showing up on a typical Sunday, even though those numbers were higher than when we began the church.

I also found it hard to write and share messages. My concussion made it hard to focus and I was jumbling my words and finding it harder and harder to concentrate.

During this time, my wife and I attended a Salvation Army officers retreat held every January. I had never been before but this year was able to make it down. During this amazing time of refreshing, God showed us a side of the Salvation Army we had not seen before. All of my preconceptions turned into misconceptions as I saw vibrant life, compassion, and love emanating from those in attendance.

While there, the Lord spoke to Sarah and she shared with me later that she felt the Lord calling us to embrace the place the Lord had given us within the Salvation Army. A month later, I felt the Lord asking me why we were still with YWAM. Don't get me wrong; it is a great organization and we treasure our time with it. But I sensed a new season ahead. We prayerfully decided it was time to end our divided heart. No more choosing between YWAM and the Salvation Army when it came to ministry involvement.

With that decision made, I also began praying about joining the Salvation Army, not just as an employee but as a committed soldier. Something I had said in the past I would never do. Not because it was wrong but because after all my experiences with organized religion, I was not ready for that kind of decision.

In the meantime, as I continued to wrestle with my post-concussion symptoms, I was finding each day a struggle. One day, while sharing with a dear friend where I was, he suggested I take a sabbatical from the church. As soon as he said this, it was like someone through a lifeline to a drowning man. I knew this was the next step in my journey.

Within a couple of months, we decided that, after five years, it was time for a break. We let the church go for the summer. I also began seeing a Christian counselor who continued to walk me through some of those past issues. It was also at this time that I began to see a brain injury support worker as well. After nine months, my symptoms lingered and I knew I needed more help.

I continued in my job, we continued looking at soldiership with the Army, and that took up most of our summer. We visited a few area churches and had regular gatherings with friends from church, but I took a true sabbatical.

Near the end of summer, I was asked to share at a local church. I said yes, and using as my text 1 Corinthians 2:3 where Paul talks about being with them in weakness, fear, and much trembling, I shared from my heart just where I was. I was not sure if I was still able to preach at this point due to my head injury struggles. By God's grace, it happened. Later, I was asked to speak to an AWANA group at a local church. I again turned to the Lord for His sustaining grace as I performed a one-man skit I had written years before. I was able to do this from memory and felt much encouraged.

You see, I still had a lesson to learn.

After coming to a deeper understanding of my identity in Christ, I had fallen back into old patterns of trying to do things in my own strength. I have often been told that I am a good public speaker, and the more that I spoke, the less I depended on God to sustain me through those times. I fell into the trap many public speakers do, relying on my own abilities instead of the Lord.

Since my head injury, I have realized once again that I can do nothing in my own strength. I can only do things through Christ who strengthens me.

*   *   *

And now we are coming full circle. We took the whole summer and prayed about our involvement with the Salvation Army. Just as we once went through the statement of faith before joining PCOG, Sarah and I now read through *Chosen to be a Soldier,* and prayerfully discussed the Army's statements of faith, doctrines, etc. We both felt the Lord calling us to this decision.

We had informed my new area commander of our decision and months later had the pleasure of becoming soldiers in the Salvation Army.

Shortly afterward, we relaunched Main Street Christian Fellowship under the covering and support of the Salvation Army. The man who once hated church was now pastoring one. The man who once hated organized religion was now part of a worldwide ministry dating back to 1865!

There is truly nothing impossible with God!

*   *   *

So there you have it—the whole long-winded, twisting, convoluted story of how one man was killed by the church. As you can see, the death wasn't physical. It was a death of emotion, of my superficial spiritual walk. I allowed circumstances and experiences to shape my identity in Christ. After the resurrection, I let my identity in Christ shape how I view the church.

You see, church isn't bad. Even our worst experiences can be redeemed by the Lord. He can heal our past, restore our present, and provide hope for our future. The question is this: will you let Him?

How does understanding our identity in Christ reshape our view of church? It goes back to perspective. I no longer look at church through the lens of my own experiences. I try to look at the church with the eyes of Christ. Do bad things happen in church? Sadly, yes. However, there is far more good that happens day in and day out. Just as the disciples, who walked with Jesus, stumbled at times, our churches still stumble today. Look though at how Jesus restored Peter after he had denied Him three times. With grace, love, and mercy, Peter was restored, given again a fresh vision to reach the lost and hurting with the love of Jesus Christ. That is my prayer for you. That is my prayer for the church.

*   *   *

Going back to the spiritual pulse I talked about in the beginning of this book, is your church operating with a healthy heartbeat?

Is Jesus Christ the main focus, or is it the law?

Are your members fellowshipping with one another?

How are people treated when caught in sin?

How does your church treat those in poverty and wealth?

Are young and old, rich and poor all allowed and encouraged to take active part in service?

Are your leaders open and transparent?

What about your own heartbeat? Where are you at in your walk with God?

Do you love the Lord with all your heart and your neighbor as yourself?

Are you working or resting?

Do you have joy?

Do you know your identity?

Are you living it out?

Only you can answer these questions.

I would encourage you to sit back and chew on these questions. Don't just give them a cursory glance. When it comes to your physical health, wisdom says to be aware of what's going on with your body. Do you ignore symptoms, or do you get things checked out? If you ignore your physical health, it *will* catch up to you. You can ignore the symptoms, but they won't always go away. Eventually, an untreated illness will cause more harm than good.

The same holds true for your spiritual health. You may be personally struggling right now with issues, fears, and doubts. If so, do you feel comfortable going to people in your church? Why not? Is it because they wouldn't be receptive? That's a sure indicator that your church may be on spiritual life-support.

However, and I want you to understand this, just because a church has problems doesn't mean you need to run away and find a new one. The problem is not the institution but the people inside. If we aren't aware and operating out of our identity in Christ, we're more apt to model unhealthy Christianity.

Remember we all have issues. We should only cast stones if we are without sin! Instead, we should come alongside those who struggle and encourage them to walk in their identity as new creations in Christ Jesus. We can't lead someone where we have not ourselves been. If you're not living in your identity, then the first step for you is to get alone with God, dig into the Word, and find out who you are!

Every church has struggles, but problems don't always indicate an unhealthy relationship with God. It would be good to remember the verse where Paul talks about his experiences of being shipwrecked, beaten, and afflicted with a host of other issues. Paul knew his identity, but he still had problems.

So to bring this together, there may be problems. No, there *will* be problems. How much of it is just the result of living in a fallen world and how much is due to us not operating out of our identity? This is where wisdom comes into play.

I will say this again: I allowed my experiences to shape my identity instead of letting Christ *be* my identity. When I realized my identity in Christ, my view of the church and my place in it changed for the better.

I pray you won't settle for anything less than the rest that can only be found in Him!

Speaking of prayer, I want to close this book by saying a prayer.

Father, I pray for those who have read this book and have been hurt by the church. I ask that You would heal their hurts, touch their heart, and bind their wounds. Help them to discover the truth of Galatians 2:20. Let them draw closer to You despite the situations they have encountered. Let them know how much You love them, care for them, and are waiting for them to let things go at the foot of the cross.

Father, for those who have not been hurt by church but have been blessed instead, I pray that You would help them to walk in grace and mercy toward those around them. If they are walking in their identity, help them to live it out by displaying Your love in action. Let them reach across denominational divides and to show love one to another.

Finally, Father, I pray that each one who reads this book will be blessed beyond measure by the power of Your love!

In the name of Jesus Christ, I pray. Amen!

ACKNOWLEDGMENTS

I know that acknowledgements are often only read by those who think they may be mentioned by the author. As this is my first book, I ask that you indulge me in this moment of thanks to those who have impacted my life and the book you now hold in your hands.

To my beautiful wife, Sarah: thank you for a lifetime of love. My life is better with you in it. Thank you for your encouragement to follow my dreams.

To my children, Hanna and Caleb: you are my blessing and my miracle. Thank you for giving Dad the space to write and for keeping me young at heart.

My parents, Bob and Barbara, and siblings, Robert and Kami, journeyed with me through the stories recorded in the first few chapters of this book. Thank you all for walking with me through those early stages.

To those friends who contributed to this book with their stories, I can only say thank-you for sharing your hearts with me. Your participation was invaluable.

In addition to those who contributed stories, other friends helped me flesh out these ideas with our numerous discussions on this and related topics. Thank you to Major Malcolm Cameron, Jim Aldrich, and Nathan and Angela Bond.

To John Armstrong: thank you for taking the time to read my initial manuscript in its entirety and for offering advice and encouragement after the fact. I have enjoyed participating in your Facebook discussions as well.

Over the years, many have encouraged me in my writing but some individuals contributed more than they will ever know. A special thank-you to those who spoke an encouraging "word in season": Vlado Psenko, Aunt Mitzie, Jim Majzel, Adrian Sandry, Rick Bell, Sean Junglas, and Tiffany Tridhardt.

Thank you as well to Ron Browning, Joe Nail, Pastor Phil Morris, Denise Morris, and Pastor Doug Anderson. Though I never told you this, you each impacted me in my journey to freedom in Christ.

I will forever be grateful to my Savior, Jesus Christ: You rescued a drowning soul and brought me safely to shore.

RECOMMENDED RESOURCES

The Salvation Army – USA: www.salvationarmyusa.org
   Canada: www.salvationarmy.ca
   International: www.salvationarmy.org
Youth With A Mission: www.ywam.org
Rising Above: www.risingabove.ca
Grace Fellowship International: www.gracefellowshipintl.com/

In addition to the Word of God, these books helped in my journey and/or were influential in other ways:

Allender, Dan. *Leading with a Limp* (Colorado Springs, Colorado: WaterBrook Press, 2006).

Apperson, Barbara. *A Sense of Destiny* (Victoria, British Columbia: Trafford, 2004).

Armstrong, John. *Your Church Is Too Small* (Grand Rapids, Michigan: Zondervan, 2010).

Buchanan, Mark. *Spiritual Rhythm* (Grand Rapids, Michigan: Zondervan, 2010).

Cavey, Bruxy. *The End of Religion* (Colorado Springs, Colorado: Navpress, 2007).

DeMoss, Nancy Leigh. *Brokenness* (Chicago, Illinois: Moody Publishers, 2002).

_____. *Surrender* (Chicago, Illinois: Moody Publishers, 2003).

_____. *Holiness* (Chicago, Illinois: Moody Publishers, 2004).

Gunderson, Denny. *The Leadership Paradox* (Seattle, Washington: YWAM Publishing, 1997).

Jackson, Anne. *Mad Church Disease* (Grand Rapids, Michigan: Zondervan, 2009).

James, Rick. *A Million Ways to Die* (Colorado Springs, Colorado: Cook, 2010).

Oberbrunner, Kary. *Your Secret Name* (Grand Rapids, Michigan: Zondervan, 2010).

Yancey, Philip. *Disappointment with God* (Grand Rapids, Michigan: Zondervan, 1988).

_____. *What's So Amazing about Grace?* (Grand Rapids, Michigan: Zondervan, 1997).

_____. *Where Is God When It Hurts?* (Grand Rapids, Michigan: Zondervan, 1990).

Feel free to visit me on the web at www.apperson.blogspot.com or send me an e-mail at rsapperson@citywest.ca.

CPSIA information can be obtained
at www.ICGtesting.com
Printed in the USA
LVOW11s1746300417
532484LV00002B/3/P